Laughing at the Gods

Any effort to understand how law works has to take seriously its main players – judges. Like any performance, judging should be evaluated by reference to those who are its best exponents. Not surprisingly, the debate about what makes a great judge is as heated and inconclusive as the debate about the purpose and nature of law itself. History shows that those who are generally considered to be candidates for a judicial hall of fame are game changers who oblige us to rethink what it is to be a good judge. So the best of judges must tread a thin line between modesty and hubris; they must be neither mere umpires nor demigods. The eight judges showcased in this book demonstrate that if the test of good judging is not about getting it right but about doing it well, then the measure of great judging is about setting new standards for what counts as judging well.

Allan C. Hutchinson is a Distinguished Research Professor at Osgoode Hall Law School at York University, Toronto, and a widely recognized leading law scholar. He is presently Dean and Associate Vice President (Graduate Studies) at York. In 2004, he was elected to the Royal Society of Canada. Hutchinson has authored or edited eighteen books, including *Is Eating People Wrong? Great Legal Cases and How They Shaped the World* (2011), *The Province of Jurisprudence Democratized* (2008), and *Evolution and the Common Law* (2005).

Laughing at the Gods

Great Judges and How They Made the Common Law

ALLAN C. HUTCHINSON

Osgoode Hall Law School, York University

CAMBRIDGE
UNIVERSITY PRESS

CAMBRIDGE UNIVERSITY PRESS
Cambridge, New York, Melbourne, Madrid, Cape Town,
Singapore, São Paulo, Delhi, Tokyo, Mexico City

Cambridge University Press
32 Avenue of the Americas, New York, NY 10013-2473, USA

www.cambridge.org
Information on this title: www.cambridge.org/9781107662766

First published 2012

Printed in the United States of America

A catalog record for this publication is available from the British Library.

Library of Congress Cataloging in Publication data

Hutchinson, Allan C., 1951–
Laughing at the gods : great judges and how they made the common law /
Allan C. Hutchinson.
  p. cm.
Includes bibliographical references and index.
ISBN 978-1-107-01726-9 (hardback) – ISBN 978-1-107-66276-6 (pbk.)
1. Judges – Biography.   2. Common law – History.   3. Judge-made law –
History.   I. Title.
K170.H88 2012
347′.0140922 – dc23   2011030607

ISBN 978-1-107-01726-9 Hardback
ISBN 978-1-107-66276-6 Paperback

This book is dedicated to the memory of my great friend and collaborator Derek Morgan (1954–2011).

Contents

Contents

Preface

This book is intended to be a loose companion to my earlier
book, *Is Eating People Wrong? Great Legal Cases and How
They Shaped the World* (2011). It takes a closer look at some
of the main characters who have stood out among the judicial
ranks and who have thereby helped to shape the world. It
is not intended as a hymn of praise for these memorable figures or the judicial function generally. Instead, it examines
the common law enterprise and seeks to identify what it is
that makes some of its judicial practitioners leaders in their
field. Whether the influence of these so-called great judges
is considered good or bad remains a question for continuing
debate. As such, this book is intended to open a conversation
about some judges and their supposed greatness.

In researching and writing this book, I have relied exten-
sively on the fine body of research that has developed over
the years about these individuals and the law. I have done
little original or primary research myself, and I have been

as comprehensive as possible in listing those sources that I have relied upon at the end of the book. I am extremely grateful to those historians and commentators.

As usual, many people have played important parts in helping me to complete this book. I have benefited from a host of critics and colleagues, mostly friendly, who have shared their time and insights. In particular, I am grateful to Rosalie Abella, Jamie Cameron, Pam Marshall, Beverly Myhal, Marilyn Pilkington, Mark Tushnet, and especially Amanda Tyler for reading earlier drafts of chapters and for preventing me from making even more startling errors and omissions. Jeannie Thomas and Albie Sachs generously allowed me to use some private photographs. However, my greatest debt is to my research assistants – Cynthia Hill set the gold standard, Jessica Diab met it with style and substance, and Ian Langlois left his own personal mark of the highest quality all over the final product.

While completing this book, I lost my longtime friend Derek Morgan. We had some of the best fun that any academic collaborators could have. Our laughter, of course, was usually at each other's expense, but it was filled with respect and affection. Although he was one of life's great contrarians, he was also at heart a simple man who wanted to be loved and cherished. I will always treasure our times together – *Thank you, my boy!*

Allan C. Hutchinson
August 2011

1

In Search of Great Judges

Playing by Their Own Rules

When the current American chief justice, John Roberts, appeared before the Senate's Judicial Committee during his confirmation hearing, he confided that he did not have an "all-encompassing approach" to his judicial role or to constitutional interpretation particularly. He went on to say that "judges are like [baseball] umpires – umpires don't make the rules; they apply them." He sealed this modest portrayal of judicial virtue by insisting that "judges have to have the humility to recognize that they operate within a system of precedent, shaped by other judges equally striving to live up to the judicial oath." The not-so-implicit message of Roberts's credo was that being a good judge required restraint and forbearance; judges, even and perhaps especially Supreme Court ones, were not in the justice game in any expansive or direct way.

Although this humble depiction of judicial responsibility – "it's my job to call balls and strikes and not to pitch or bat" – will strike a reassuring chord with many, it fails to understand the history and nature of the judicial role in common law countries. That is, if the acknowledged pantheon of great judges is anything to go by, judges are much more than umpires. Any proposed list of candidates for a judicial hall of fame is far from being characterized by those judges' self-understanding or by an essentially passive and restrained performance of their role. To paraphrase T.S. Eliot, if immature judges follow and mature judges lead, then great judges blaze entirely fresh trails.

The analogy between judging and umpiring is misleading and inaccurate. As far as their common law duties go in both constitutional and nonconstitutional matters, history demonstrates that judges are very much part of the action. It is less about *whether* they change the rules than about *how* they do so. In the last few hundred years of its lifespan, the law has changed, and judges have been some of the main architects and artisans of that change. Staying with the baseball analogy, whereas some umpires claim to call balls and strikes "as they see 'em," others assert that "they ain't nothin' 'til I call 'em." People might be fated to play a baseball game of the judges' choosing, but the judges are also very much part of the game; they play by as well as change the rules as they go along. In legal terms, not only what counts as "balls" and "strikes" but also what counts as "baseball" changes over time. And it is the judges, for better and worse, who are the purveyors and guardians of these changes.

That being said, if judges are not umpires, neither are they godly figures. They have no special, let alone sacred, insight into the meaning of legal texts or the nature of social justice – judgeliness is not next to godliness. Just as there is no way to simply read off the meaning of laws, especially constitutions, in an impersonal exercise of professional technique without resort to larger and contested issues of social and political values, there is also no way for judges to negotiate that fraught terrain with a quasi-divine certainty or supernatural wisdom. As Francis Bacon observed, "whoever undertakes to set himself up as a judge of Truth and Knowledge is shipwrecked by the laughter of the gods." This is a major caution for those who aspire to greatness. Some appreciate the risk and succeed in being great (and some even occasionally laugh at themselves). But others are not so vigilant and court godly derision, as they believe their own hype and lose an appropriate sense of perspective; these contenders are often condemned to a watery grave.

Indeed, there is much to be said for taking judges less seriously than lawyers, and perhaps judges themselves often do. Indeed, this book runs the considerable risk of committing exactly that fault in courting the idea of there being so-called great judges. Greatness is a quality that tends too easily to intimate a superhuman capacity or achievement; critics and commentators also chance the shipwrecking laughter of the gods. Consequently, a respect for judges should be tempered with a little irreverence. Peter Cook of *Beyond the Fringe* (a celebrated English satirical revue of the 1960s) offered a suitably humorous reminder of this in his memorable character of a working-class man:

> Yes, I could have been a judge but I never had the Latin, never had the Latin for the judgin', I never had it, so I'd had it, as far as bein' a judge was concerned. I just never had sufficient of it to get through the rigourous judging exams and so I became a miner instead. I'd rather have been a judge than a miner. Being a miner, as soon as you are too old and tired and sick and stupid to do the job properly, you have to go. Well, the very opposite applies with judges.

The general problem is not whether or not any judge *ought* to be "a judge of Truth and Knowledge." The fact of the matter is that they *are* treated as if they *do* have that power. Many common law jurisdictions, like Canada, the United States, and lately the United Kingdom, have bestowed that enormous and elevated power on them. Although this may not have been a deliberate decision and may even run counter to the traditional defense of judicial propriety, judges wield enormous power and are often accorded exaggerated respect in their professional capacity to intuit "Truth and Knowledge." Whether or not the gods like it and whether or not they are laughing are almost beside the point. Sometimes mutedly and sometimes uproariously, the judges are effectively laughing right back at them. By personal undertaking or institutional insistence, great judges are thrust into the political business of "Truth and Knowledge" (or, more pointedly, Justice). And, as is often the case, the joke is on society as much as on anyone else.

So judges, even great ones, are neither heavenly saints nor sporting officials. Those who chance greatness must strive to tread a thin line between an unconvincing modesty (i.e., does anyone really believe that judges are or can be compared to baseball umpires?) and a precious hubris (i.e., does anyone really believe that judges are anything more than ordinary mortals doing a difficult and demanding job?). Judging is by nature an audacious task; however, it is not necessarily the most audacious who are recognized as great. Robert Jackson, a justice of the American Supreme Court, hit the right note when he famously stated that "we are not final because we are infallible, we are infallible because we are final." The last word is not the only word or the best word.

So what is involved in judging? And what distinguishes a great judge from a merely very good one? Of course, the debate over what makes a great judge and which judicial personalities should be included among the hallowed numbers of great judges is as heated and as divisive as any other in the jurisprudential literature. Nevertheless, the obvious difficulties of arriving at any neutral or uncommitted account of what makes a great judge and who should be included in this hypothetical judicial hall of fame have not managed to dissuade lawyers and jurists from engaging in such an exercise. Indeed, developing lists of the essential qualities that great judges should possess and determining which judges meet such exalted standards has become something of a jurisprudential parlor game.

It should come as no surprise that this debate over great judges is as contested as the broader engagement over the nature and purpose of law and adjudication more generally – the two are connected in obvious and inextricable ways. The particular standards of what counts as a paradigmatic example of good judging will be informed by the protagonist's commitment to a particular theory of law and adjudication. For instance, whether judges are to be praised for their technical expertise, their political acumen, or both will largely depend on the background understanding about the task in which the judges are supposed to be engaged and the resources that they are expected to utilize. Those with a more positivistic account of what law is (i.e., that there is or should be some important differentiation between the existence of legal rules and their moral merit) will laud very different traits from those with a more naturalist orientation (i.e., that there is and should be a tight connection between the existence of legal rules and their moral worth). Fraught with difficulties and disagreements, the debate in and around great judges is simply one more intellectual location for further engagement over what law is and is supposed to be.

For example, a classic and esteemed effort to identify judicial greatness is made by Henry J. Abraham. He offers a list of the top ten qualities of a great American judge to which all judges should aspire and that a small handful of judges actually do embody. For him, whereas Hugo Black and Lewis Powell make the cut, Thurgood Marshall and Learned Hand do not. Although Abraham's list contains many predictable qualities (e.g., craftsmanship, personal integrity, and proper training) that most observers would accept, it also includes a number of question-begging requirements (e.g., demonstrated judicial temperament, absolute fair-mindedness, and a solid understanding of the proper judicial role of judges under the Constitution) that go to the very heart of the debate over what makes a judge great and, by implication, what the judicial task is all about. Moreover, there is no particular reason to think that the qualities of a great American judge will necessarily be the same as those of other jurisdictions. Although there will obviously be some substantial overlap, the demands of one society's legal system and its civic expectations might manifest themselves in a significantly different set of vaunted judicial qualities.

But the main problem is that Abraham's criteria do not so much provide answers to the problem posed, but simply rephrase the main questions to be answered. Determining what counts as "demonstrated judicial temperament" and "a solid understanding of the proper judicial role of judges under the Constitution" is the very stuff of jurisprudential debate. Unless you subscribe to some Platonic notion that "essence or true existence are always what they are, having the same simple self-existent and unchanging forms, not admitting of variation at all, in any way, at any time," the qualities of judicial greatness are historically contingent; they shift and change over time. There is no one set of qualities that define a great judge. Like beauty and goodness, greatness is an ideal that is always on the move. Prevailing conceptions of greatness are simply the currently unchallenged but soon-to-be-resisted markers for a working consensus that was temporarily reached.

A sampling of judicial biographies reveals that they are as much about the appropriate criteria by which to assess judicial achievement as they are about the particular judge under scrutiny. In a recent biography on another American titan, Billings Learned Hand, Gerald Gunther compares him with another reputed colossus of the American legal scene, Oliver Wendell Holmes Jr. In touting the virtues of Learned Hand over Holmes, he argues less that Learned Hand has the qualities of a great judge than that the qualities of a great judge are defined by and embodied in Learned Hand. Although Learned Hand's judicial record is marked by "disinterestedness and lack of crusading zeal," this did not condemn him to intellectual impotence, because, according to Gunther, "his decisions were noted for . . . superior craftsmanship and for creative performance within the confines set by the executive and legislative branches." In campaigning to include a judge on the list of undisputed great judges, biographers shape as much as respond to the conditions of membership. "Greatness" is itself revealed as a crafted quality, not a naturally assumed distinction or enduring status.

Any effort to locate the essential and enduring qualities of a great judge, therefore, will be very much a function of the view that the list maker has of what law is. For me, the common law is a dynamic and engaged activity in which how judges deal with rules is considered as vital as the resulting content of the rules and actual decisions made; judges are social artisans of the first order whose impact, although often more subtle and understated than their political counterparts, is undeniable. The common law is better understood less as a fixed body of rules and regulations than as a living judicial tradition of dispute resolution. Because law is a social practice and society is in a constant state of agitated movement, law is always an organic and hands-on practice that is never the complete or finished article; it is always situated inside and within, not outside and beyond, the society in which it arises. In short, the common law is a *work in progress* – evanescent, dynamic, productive, tantalizing, untidy, and bottom-up: it is more tentative than teleological, more inventive than orchestrated, more fabricated than formulaic, and more pragmatic than perfected.

Having this experimental, catch-as-catch-can, and anything-might-go sense about it, the common law recommends that its judicial personnel also adopt some of those qualities. Although it is clearly a great help to possess an excellent set of technical skills, these will not be enough in and of themselves; they are a necessary but not sufficient condition of greatness. The battery of adjudicative techniques for rule application does not amount to a self-contained or self-operating technology: the techniques only make sense as part of a larger understanding of law as a rhetorical and dynamic enterprise. Being a practical activity, adjudication does not consist of a series of formulaic applications in an abstract space. Instead, it is more profitably understood as an organic and judgment-based engagement in real time and in real places; it is less an occasion for logical operations than an exercise in operational logic.

Nonetheless, although the learned knack of using legal materials with adroitness and dexterity is not to be under-rated, the effect of such a limited depiction of lawyers' special and distinctive expertise is misleading. It can too easily be used to avoid the democratic responsibility of justifying judicial power and authority by reference to the real-world pressure of getting the job done. The depiction of the judicial craft as an inward and insular undertaking serves to cut off law and adjudication from the sustaining sociopolitical context and rich historical resources from which they gain their vigor. Legal artistry demands more than technical proficiency. The best judicial craftspersons are not those who simply reproduce mechanically and mindlessly old arguments and trite analogies; they are those who can rework legal materials in an imaginative and stylish way. A bare legal craft can too easily acquire the elite habits of a Masonic order and fail to meet or sabotage its civic obligations: a job well done is not always its own reward.

To be worthy of the highest professional prestige, lawyers and judges must nurture a sense of social justice and a feel for political vision. Without these qualities, they will more likely become only hired hands for vested interests. As one commentator succinctly put it, "technique without ideals is a menace; ideals without technique are a mess." Adjudication is not carpentry. Although judges would do well to inculcate an equivalent judicial pride in their work, they also must be designers and innovators who place their professional craft in the service of political values and social ideals. It is true that legal tables will wobble and precedential doors will jam without crafted care and professional attention, but there is a significant difference between the doors and tables of a torture chamber and those of a hospital ward; a hospital bed is not a torture rack, although it can become one. Values and commitments can be hidden, but they cannot be done away with altogether. Judges and jurists cannot so easily evade taking responsibility for the artifacts and outcomes of their crafted performances by taking refuge in matters of technical consistency and internal coherence. In the same way that a block of wood has only whatever shape and symmetry that it happened to pick up at the last turn of the carpenter's lathe, the law possesses only whatever shape and symmetry that it happened to acquire during the last occasion for legal crafting.

It should not be surprising, therefore, that my sense of what it is to be a great judge is not about the stereotypical rule follower or skilled technician. Instead (and history is squarely on my side in this), I maintain that a great judge is someone who does not go with the flow; someone who is something of a maverick, a go-it-alone person who works across the grain. This does not mean that great judges do what they wish when they wish; they must be able to convince and carry some of their colleagues along with them, at least some of the way. As one judge and scholar has noted, the common law tradition assigns to judges "a creative role in improving law, as well as a guardian's role in preserving its continuity and predictability." It is the ability to combine these tasks – creating and preserving – in a convincing whole that marks a judge as a candidate for judicial greatness. To achieve this across a full career and not merely in occasional cases is a formidable challenge.

Across the common law world and its extensive history, the ranks of great judges are small in number. In the words of one putative great judge, these are "bold spirits" who can imagine different and more ennobling ways to do what they do: they make the rank-and-filers, including the most talented, appear as if "timorous souls" who are, in comparison, too afraid or too hidebound to glimpse, let alone grasp, these hidden opportunities. So Chief Justice Roberts is unlikely to join the list of great judges if he stays close to his notion of the good judge as humble umpire. In contrast, great judges seem to have technical skills in abundance, but they also possess a less common vision and a playfulness that makes them stand out. And, as importantly, they recognize the imperative to place their personal craft in the service of the greater values and ideals of the larger enterprise in which they find themselves.

The qualities of great judges are much the same as that of so-called great people. Although there is obviously no fixed set of qualities that such people have or an agreed list of who deserves inclusion among these select few, there are some general observations that can be made. In particular, apart from compiling an enviable record of vast achievement and impact, such people share one particular attribute: the insistence on doing it their own way. Although from different backgrounds and with different personal characteristics, great people are not only prepared to swim against the social or political tide, but they also manage to turn the tide partly their way and carry people along with them. It is as much about how they do it as what they do.

The hallmark of these people (be they artists, athletes, politicians, philosophers, or judges) is that they are consummate performers. What makes them great is not simply their ability to beat everyone at their own game; it is the capacity to envision and dictate a different game to be played. Greatness is to be found in an inestimable genius for improvising and transforming conventional standards. For such people, the best accolades are earned not for their technical prowess, but for their capacity to reveal possibilities that others have not even seen or thought viable. Those people have left their mark on the world because they have, in the best sense of the phrase, understood that "dealing with great tasks as play . . . is a sign of greatness." Great players are not those who simply play well or exhibit a flawless technique. They are those people who take the world by the scruff of its neck and shake it until it becomes something more amenable to their own influence.

Most important, greatness requires vision and inventiveness that are matched by having the courage of one's convictions; a certain stubbornness and single-mindedness is a trait of many great people. What made Mahatma Gandhi, Elizabeth I, Nelson Mandela, Golda Meir, Martin Luther King Jr., and Albert Einstein into great people was their belief that their lasting impact would be not simply their particular achievements, but their shining example, which would light up the path of others as they walked forward into the challenges of a shadowy future. Their ultimate message was not simply to do what they did. Their greatness was in embodying a particular attitude and temperament. By dint of their attitude and ability, they wanted to make the world a better place by creating hope in a brighter future and by endowing others with opportunities to remake their own world.

And so it is with great judges. They are not afraid to take a stance and will not always get it right. But they insist that they do things their own way. Even if their views do not always prevail or carry the day entirely, they manage by dint of their example and efforts to change the legal world and the way others think about the judicial role. A special facility for deploying the traditional skills and techniques of the judicial craft is central to being able to assume such a stance, but these skills and techniques are not sufficient in themselves. Indeed, at their most successful, such great judges rework and supplement what are considered to be the traditional skills and requisite techniques of judicial accomplishment. Great judges accept that there is no method or manifesto in the sense of a process that can be followed that will produce and vouchsafe particular results; great judging is as much an attitude and a temperament as anything else. Great judges oblige us to rethink what it is to be a good judge.

Such great judges play with and through the extant rules. Grasping an institutional responsibility to experiment in reasonable and reasoned ways, they tend to take a pragmatic attitude toward the meaning and merit of past decisions; they recognize that another current way of understanding the past is to imagine a better future. Great judges seek to make a critical accommodation with the legal tradition by combining heresy and heritage in a playful judicial style; they refuse to be hampered by customary habits of judicial mind. For them, law is not something to be mastered. It is a sprawling tableau of transformation in which experimentation and improvisation are valued as much as predictability and faithfulness to existing rules and ideas. They see possibilities and make moves that others overlook. Great judges flaunt conventional standards in the process of remaking them; their judgments are the exceptions that prove the rule. And, once they have done what they do, others are less able to view the world in the same way again.

At their most audacious, great judges take an almost daredevilish approach; this is done not out of a couldn't-care-less frivolousness, but from a deep commitment to their own sense of what is right. In doing so, they demonstrate not only a willingness to chance spectacular failure, but also the courage to court it; it is a precarious and potent recipe for greatness that only a few can even aspire to, let alone successfully achieve. Such players must, by definition, be few and far between. Yet it is their occasional explosion onto the judicial scene that lights up the legal and social world and allows people to see as workaday and ordinary what was previously thought extraordinary and exemplary. In this way, great judges change existing standards as they exceed them. As such, great judges succeed most when they are praised not so much for the legal soundness of their work, but for the sit-up-and-take-notice boldness of their interventions.

By these standards, a great judge is far from being one who "got it right" in the sense that, whatever the immediate reaction to a particular decision or their careers, they managed to strike on the correct result in terms of political progress or social justice. But great judges are those who stirred the prevailing pot of received wisdom and, even if they did not always succeed, confronted people with a different take on the world. Indeed, a number of judges were clearly far from consistent in the political cut of their opinions. Of course, there had to be a considerable or workable overlap between their judgments and what was perceived as socially desirable, or else their worth as a decent judge, let alone a great one, would be questionable. You can only swim against the tide for so long. At some point, you need to pull others along with you and persuade them to turn the tide.

Whether in law or other areas of human achievement, debates about greatness are irresolvable. They cannot be conclusively settled by resort to some objective algorithm that will provide proof positive of any assessment. However, what can be done is to clarify the preferences and prejudices that are in play and to try to build a series of common agreements from which to move on to more contentious matters. Despite what many experts and authorities insist, there is no solid ground on which to stand, only the shifting and shaky ground of half-sensed and half-articulated beliefs. Whether we are evaluating people or judges, there is no final or indisputable basis for judgment; there is only and always the mutual game of argument and persuasion – whether Ronald Reagan and Margaret Thatcher were great political leaders is not a matter of objective assessment but implicates much that is contested about politics and leadership. So it is in law and with great judges. The beauty of legal criticism is that such matters of greatness cannot be resolved; they call us back and constitute the stuff that makes the pursuits of law, justice, and life as tantalizing, as compelling, and as important as they are.

Have I set the standard so high that no one can meet its exacting requirements? My answer is a definite no. There is a small group of common law judges across the world and centuries that are eligible for the imprimatur of greatness and, by my lights, fully deserving of that accolade; they have left their mark on the legal process by changing our understanding of what it means to be a great judge. In compiling my definition of greatness and list of great judges, I have flitted back and forth between the development of general criteria and the inclusion of judges who are almost universally recognized as great judges. Any listing that did not include Tom Denning or John Marshall would surely miss the mark. Accordingly, I have striven to locate a reflective equilibrium, albeit precarious and controversial, between general conventions about who is a great judge and my own vision of what is involved in fulfilling the adjudicative demands of the common law. Of course, the result reflects some of my own prejudices and preferences, but it is not entirely reducible to them.

Not surprisingly, I insist that the octet of judges that I have selected can all lay claim to possessing that elusive quality of greatness that I have begun to sketch. Although there are others who might reasonably be accorded the accolade of judicial greatness (Brian Dickson in Canada and Owen Dixon in Australia, to name but two), my chosen eight represent a first and defensible effort at the task. That said, I believe that those who made the cut have played the judicial game in such a singular way that their contribution helped to transform how people thought about the adjudicative role as well as reacted to the law itself. And, in most cases, their influence persists well beyond their immediate historical context; they are still talked about today. In short, they performed as "revolutionaries" whose impact on law and adjudicative standards has not been dimmed by time and change – baseball umpires they are most decidedly not. Of course, my selections will be challenged, as will my criteria for greatness. But it is in the nature of such inquiries to stimulate, not settle, debates about judicial greatness.

2

Lord Mansfield

A Long Journey

Like so much else that he wrote, Shakespeare's comments on greatness strike a resonant chord – "In my stars I am above thee; but be not afraid of greatness: some are born great, some achieve greatness, and some have greatness thrust upon 'em." But he gives us very little hint of what greatness might be. Indeed, it is an elusive quality that defies easy or obvious clarification. Like the setting of Shakespeare's words in *Twelfth Night*, it is a many-layered concept whose meaning takes on shape and color depending on its context. In the play, although Malvolio says the words, they are in fact contained in a letter that is part of an elaborate ruse by Maria, who composes the letter in Olivia's hand. Similarly, greatness is very much a quality that shifts and reconstitutes itself as circumstances demand. Being great is as much about setting the defining terms as about meeting them.

One of those judges who can lay a relatively uncontroversial claim to greatness is the eighteenth-century Lord Mansfield; he aligned the common law more closely to the pursuit of substantive justice. He was at ground zero of the early efforts to construct the modern foundations of the common law. As long as some allowance is made for the immediate conditions and historical constraints under which he worked, he has been anointed as the very model of a great judge – his claim to greatness has not only withstood the test of time but also been bolstered by it. Consequently, the challenge is not to make the case for Mansfield's inclusion in the ranks of great judges, but to inquire into and identify what made him great. In doing so, we might be able to get a better handle on the qualities of greatness that have motivated most lawyers and others in their assessments of later judges.

In 1718, a thirteen-year-old William Murray made the trip south from east Scotland to London in order to enroll as a student at Westminster School. Riding alone for most of the journey, without any family companions, the trip covered about four hundred miles and took him almost eight weeks to complete. It was the beginning of a journey that was to take him all the way to the very pinnacle of English politics and law; he was never to return to Scotland in his remaining seventy-five years. As this anecdote suggests, this was a very different time than our own – the Industrial Age had not yet dawned; slavery and a brutal criminal code were the order of the day; the United States did not yet exist; and universal suffrage was a subversive pipe dream. It was Murray's destiny as the future Lord Mansfield to make a huge impact on a century that was itself one of enormous transformation and change. As both lawyer and politician, he can reasonably be named as one of the pivotal figures of the eighteenth-century world – his was a trip of enormous importance and influence for the common law and society at large.

William was born on 2 March 1705. He was the fourth of fourteen children born to the fifth Viscount Stormont and his wife, Margaret. Their home and William's birthplace was Scone Palace, which had been the ceremonial home of Scottish kings for many centuries (and also the coronation site of Shakespeare's fictional Macbeth). As long-established members of the Scottish aristocracy, the family members were traditionally supporters of the Jacobite cause who remained loyal to the deposed Stuart lineage of the English Crown, not the reigning House of Hanover. This was an issue that would dog William for much of his English career.

Blessed with talent and opportunity, William was a bright young lad. He began his schooling at the local Perth Grammar School. Ironically, his Scottish education gave him an edge over his English counterparts because, although they studied only Greek and Latin, William was obliged to learn the intricacies of English grammar. However, it was clear that William was a student of genuine academic promise and that he would fare much better if he continued his schooling south of the border. So, at the tender age of thirteen, he traveled to London to enroll in Westminster School, where he distinguished himself as a King's Scholar. When he was eighteen, he gained a place as a commoner at Christ Church College at Oxford University. A student of intelligence and industry, he excelled himself as a prize-winning scholar in history and classics and became fluent in French. With the harsh burr of his Scottish brogue now partly smoothed off, William graduated with some distinction in 1727 and set off to make a professional life for himself in London.

William was determined to become a barrister (an advocate), but his Scottish background and distinct lack of funds stood in his path. Two events fortuitously combined to clear his way to a legal career. In the summer of 1727, not long after George I's demise, William won a competition to write a eulogistic poem in Latin entitled *The Death of the King*; a fellow entrant was William Pitt (a future Whig politician and leader), with whom William was to joust throughout their careers. Not only did this victory bring William to public attention, but it also confirmed his credentials as a loyal supporter of the Hanoverian monarchy; his perceived Jacobite tendencies were effectively, if only temporarily, stilled. In addition, it had the desired effect of securing the patronage of Baron Thomas Foley (whose son, Thomas, was

Detail of engraving of Alexander Pope by Jacobus Houbraken, 1747. *Source:* Harvard Art Museums/Fogg Museum, Gift of William Gray from the collection of Francis Calley Gray, G1996. Imaging Department © President and Fellows of Harvard College.

a school friend of William's); he bestowed on William a generous annual allowance of £200. Subsequently well placed and well funded, he joined Lincoln's Inn (one of the colleges that young lawyers had to join) and began his pupillage (apprenticeship) under the supervision of William Hamilton, the first truly Scottish advocate at the English bar. After a few years of study and apprenticeship, William Murray was called to the bar (became a lawyer) on 23 November 1730. He secured a place in chambers (law offices) at 5 King's Bench

Walk in the Temple, the Christopher Wren–designed heart of legal London.

Around this time, William made the friendship of the celebrated poet Alexander Pope. In a short time, he took a paternal role in William's life and gave him the social standing and connections that any aspiring young man of the time needed. Indeed, Pope paid Murray the considerable compliment of writing a poem about him, "Ode to Venus." William had taken a shine to a beautiful young woman, but his romantic ambitions were thwarted by her parents, who judged William to be insufficiently endowed to be a suitable match for their daughter. As few lawyers have been immortalized before or since, Murray's romantic plight became the stuff of literature:

> To Number Five direct your doves,
> There spread round Murray all your blooming loves;
> Noble and young, who strikes the heart
> With every sprightly, every decent part;
> Equal the injured to defend,
> To charm the mistress, or to fix the friend.
> He, with a hundred arts refined,
> Shall stretch thy conquests over half the kind:
> To him each rival shall submit,
> Make but his riches equal to his wit.
> Then shall thy form the marble grace
> (Thy Grecian form), and Chloe lend the face.

William parlayed his Scottish contacts and background into a successful legal career. His big break came in 1733, when he was still a relatively young thirty-year-old lawyer. He managed to be briefed on several Scottish appeals from the Court of Sessions to the House of Lords (the United Kingdom's highest court). However, his career really began to take off in 1737. Following some murderous riots in Edinburgh, Parliament had decided to disenfranchise the entire city. Murray was retained as one of the counsel for the city and was able to mollify substantially the reprisals ultimately imposed. He was awarded the Freedom of the City of Edinburgh for his fine work, and this cemented his reputation as a definite one to be watched in both law and politics. A year later, in 1738, Murray defended William Sloper in a scandalous case in which Sloper was being sued for having an affair with the wife of a renowned comedian, Colley Cibber. In mounting a successful defense, he displayed a legal sophistication and social sensitivity that recommended him to both legal and popular opinion makers.

At around this time, William also met his future wife, Lady Elizabeth Finch. It was a good match both socially and personally. She was the daughter of the Earl of Winchelsea, and they were married on 20 September 1738 at Raby Castle in County Durham. Although they were unable to have children, they seemed to remain happily married for forty-six years, until her death in 1784. With a wife and solid social standing, everything was now in place for William Murray to build on his professional successes and make an even greater splash in the institutional pools of midcentury England.

1742 was a banner year for William Murray. A freshly minted king's counsel, he had long harbored ambitions of obtaining public office. However, he had little appetite for party politics. This was a definite dilemma, as most government positions of the time demanded political affiliation. Fortunately, William had become closely acquainted with the powerful Duke of Newcastle, a titan of English politics. When the position of solicitor general (who operated under the attorney general and was tasked with advising the government and cabinet on all legal matters) became vacant, he accepted a patronage appointment as the member of Parliament for the Yorkshire constituency of Boroughbridge, which was under the duke's control. Murray distinguished himself in this post; he burnished his already glowing reputation with his astute ability to keep his political leanings separate from his legal opinions. He negotiated several tricky situations. In 1747, he helped to prepare legislation to abolish most hereditary entitlements in Scotland. Also, after putting to rest official suspicions about his possible Jacobite sympathies, he led the treason prosecution of the Jacobite aristocrats who supported the Scottish pretender prince Charles Stuart in his rebellion against England at the 1746 battle of Culloden Field; the defendants were the last to be beheaded on London's Tower Hill.

On the appointment of Sir Dudley Ryder to the lord chief judgeship in 1754, Murray was appointed as his successor as attorney general. This gave formal confirmation to the already accepted fact that Murray was the government's leading legal voice and advisor. In the same year, he declined an offer to become the Master of the Rolls (who at the time was deputy to the Lord Chancellor) in the hope that he would soon be appointed to the more prestigious position of Lord Chief Justice of the Court of King's Bench. In a couple of years, history and the incumbent Chief Justice duly obliged. Ryder died and, despite inducements by the government for him to remain attorney general (including the chancellorship of the Duchy of Lancaster for life and a substantial allowance), Murray was appointed in his place. On taking office in November 1756, he received a peerage and became Baron Mansfield; this was later to be enhanced to Earl of Mansfield in 1776. He was then England's most senior judge. In a position of real power, he was able to start leaving his own distinct imprint on both law and government.

During this period and for most of his remaining career, Mansfield continued to play an active part in politics and be involved in Parliament's legislative work. He was also widely considered the best and most "silver-tongued" speaker in Parliament; Pope's influence and instruction had paid ample dividends. This was fully on display in his political and oratorical rivalry with William Pitt. So personal was the animosity between the two that Murray refused to attend Pitt's funeral in May 1778. In a practice that is now largely alien to most students of government, he became a cabinet minister in 1757, while still serving as Lord Chief Justice, and continued as a cabinet member until

1763; Montesquieu's famous doctrine of 'the separation of powers' had not yet taken a very strong hold. Indeed, for a brief period, Mansfield also served as Chancellor of the Exchequer and Speaker of the House of Lords; this was a combination of roles that created the kind of conflict of interest that the more strict American arrangement of constitutional affairs would later firmly reject. However, even though he was repeatedly offered the Lord Chancellorship, he declined. Although the Chancellorship lacked any secure tenure or reliable compensation, the office of Chief Justice offered both. Notwithstanding his aristocratic achievements, Mansfield's arrival in London as an impecunious young Scottish émigré had left a deep and enduring mark.

As Lord Chief Justice, Lord Mansfield was to serve for more than thirty years and to become in some observers' assessment not only "the legal genius of his generation," but also "the greatest common law judge." Edmund Burke referred him to as "that great light of the law." Mansfield took full advantage of his wide set of talents – legal expertise, oratorical fluency, personal charm, unflagging energy, and political judgment – and deployed them in a timely and effective manner. In particular, he recognized the need for the law to keep up with the increasing pace of commercial and mercantile change. In an age in which law and politics were not yet perceived as distant relatives, he strived to ensure that the common law was something to be admired, not tolerated or finessed. As he said when arguing a case as solicitor general, he sought to ensure that "the common law . . . works itself pure by rules drawn from the fountain of justice." It is not only his own success at remaining true to this view that marks him for greatness, but that he urged this view on others and persuaded later generations of judges to follow his lead. There are definite echoes of Mansfield's approach in the work of Lord Atkin (see Chapter 5). Indeed, even twenty-first-century scholars, like Ronald Dworkin, invoke his example in their laudatory accounts of the common law process.

Although Mansfield was an English-trained lawyer and judge, he developed an approach to his judicial duties that smacked of the civilian method. Whether this was because of his lingering Scottish affiliations (Scotland has a more Roman-derived tradition of law) is unclear. But he saw the judge's responsibility to be as much about formulating legal principles as about following legal rules. Nevertheless, he was not cavalier about existing precedents. With dexterity and rigor, he would draw on existing rulings but interpret and reshape them to suit what he saw as the most desirable outcomes. As he said in *Fisher v. Prince* in 1762, "the reason and spirit of cases make law; not the letter of particular precedents." This approach was helped by the fact that law reporting was still in a very rudimentary state, and the reliability of earlier reported judgments was suspect. Nevertheless, there were times when he accepted that the need for certainty in the law outweighed the urge to do justice in the individual case. Like many other great judges, he knew that discretion was occasionally the better part of valor.

Although Mansfield's more expansive judicial style is hardly considered novel or original today, its innovative and almost groundbreaking quality at the time cannot be exaggerated. Judges tended to see themselves as operating under more prosaic restrictions than the poetic Mansfield would allow. He was unafraid to irrigate the dry soil of legal rules with more invigorating waters. For instance, in *Trueman v. Fenton* in 1777, he opined that "I never like to entangle justice in matters of form and to turn parties around upon frivolous objections where I can avoid it – it only tends to the ruin and destruction of both." Consequently, Mansfield believed not that he was making new law but that he was liberating the real and abiding principles of the common law from the enchainment of earlier mistaken characterizations. As he put it in *Pugh v. Duke of Leeds* in the same year, the proper judicial task was "not to make new law, but to vindicate the old from misrepresentation." Although he did not go so far as to declare that unjust rules could not be law (as some of his later judicial heirs, like Tom Denning, have done), he did work his hardest to make law and justice coalesce.

In attempting to forge a more seamless alliance between law and justice, Mansfield relied on a couple of favorite techniques that have been vindicated by the tests of time and experience. The first involved a resort to equitable principles. Mansfield's judicial tenure came before the courts of law and equity were combined into a single court in England almost a century later, in the 1870s. At the time, equitable claims were still made before the Lord Chancellor of the Court of Chancery. However, a favorite technique of Mansfield's was to rely preemptively on the rules of equity in the Court of King's Bench. Although this got him into hot water with judges and critics, like Jeremy Bentham, he made light of such naysayers and adopted an approach that made him very much a man ahead of his time. For him, the effort to detach law from equity or justice was as wrongheaded as it was unnecessary.

The second technique was the use of so-called legal fictions. At this stage in its development, the common law contained some embedded, awkward concepts that were ill suited to the changing nature of society and commerce. Mansfield became a master at utilizing the device of positing certain debatable matters as fact so that existing rules could be applied more favorably in difficult or unanticipated situations. He did this in his game-changing effort to establish the foundations of modern commercial law. For instance, he would treat paper property (share certificates, annuities, etc.) as actual forms of property to protect developing trading interests. Part of the impetus for this was that Mansfield, following Blackstone, maintained that this was a more reliable way to update the law than leaving it to the partisan whims of Parliament. In this way, he was able to

Lord Mansfield, Chief Justice of the Court of King's Bench. Painted by William Russell Birch, 1785. *Source:* Courtesy of Historical & Special Collections, Harvard Law School Library.

stitch a more accurate picture of commercial practice into the tradition-bound fabric of the common law. For many, this creative exercise of judicial initiative was a hallmark of Mansfield's genius.

Both of these innovative techniques evidenced Mansfield's informing approach about the relationship between the common law and legislation. He was an unabashed champion of the view that much legal reform was better and more expeditiously achieved through the courts than through legislative assemblies. In taking this stance, he gave life to an attitude and posture that remains the stuff of contemporary controversy. He insisted that the animating justice of the common law was "exclusive of positive law enacted by statute." So that, by virtue of its capacity for "working itself pure," the common law could claim to be "superior to an act of parliament." Whereas this was a convenient as well as insightful stance for someone who at the time occupied the judicial bench rather than the political seats of Parliament, it has become for better and worse the received view among judges and jurists. Although legislation is accepted as being institutionally superior to the common law, its impact and influence is limited to the precise terms and range of its enactment. It is Mansfield's continuing (and, some would say, dubious) legacy that more than two centuries of judges have followed his example and treated the common law as possessing a deep wisdom that far exceeds the cobbled-together political compromises of legislators.

In advancing this strategy, Mansfield made sure that he cultivated the support of academic scholars. When Mansfield became a lawyer and then a judge, Edward Coke's seventeenth-century texts, *Institutes* and *Reports*, were very much the authoritative sources of the common law. However, much of this learning was not to Mansfield's taste. So he placed his considerable clout behind the growing reputation of a man named William Blackstone. Younger than

Mansfield, Blackstone had been called to the bar in 1746 but had made no strong impression. Instead, Blackstone gave a series of private lectures at Oxford on the laws and government of England. Perhaps surprisingly, this was a novel approach and challenged the prevailing ascendancy of Roman law and learning in the universities. Having rattled the educational establishment, Blackstone's route to scholarly respectability seemed blocked.

Utilizing his extensive network of political and academic contacts, Mansfield was supportive in having Blackstone appointed to the newly created Vinerian Chair at Oxford in 1758 (which remains the University's leading chair). In the next few years, Blackstone completed his monumental *Commentaries on the Laws of England*, which he first published from 1765 to 1769. Although Mansfield did not agree with all of Blackstone's summaries, he was partial to his overall views and approach. Indeed, there was a fruitful exchange of opinions between Mansfield and Blackstone over the years; Blackstone incorporated many of Mansfield's opinions, especially his conception of consideration based on Mansfield's judgment in *Pillans* (see later discussion), into his later editions and revisions. They served together for a short time in 1770 on the Court of King's Bench. Both being opinionated and strong willed, it was not a happy partnership.

Although Mansfield did not convert everyone to his transformative approach, an indication of his dominance can be gleaned from the fact that, in his first thirteen years on the bench, there were no dissenting judgments from his colleagues in his cases. And, by the time he retired, there were only about twenty in total; the House of Lords only reversed him on six appeals. This is an astonishing record. Although it might be largely attributable to his institutional position, this record also has something to do with his intellectual authority. In the first dissent, in *Millar v. Taylor* in 1769, he went out of his way to note that "unanimity never could have happened if we did not among ourselves communicate our sentiments with great freedom; if we did not form our judgments without any prepossession to first thoughts; if we were not always open to conviction and ready to yield to each other's reasons." This concession says much about the persuasive and collegial skills of Mansfield as judge and chief justice.

On his appointment as Lord Chief Justice, Mansfield realized that, if he were to shake up the content of English law, he would first have to make the procedural side of law more conducive to change. He introduced a series of reforms that would streamline the performance of the courts. In particular, he broke the hold that senior barristers had on the business of the courts: he changed the pleading order so that more and better motions were brought forward. He also did away with the time-consuming practice of reserving most judgments. In a practice that still prevails in the English courts, judgments were delivered, often extemporaneously, at the end of the case. However, although these institutional reforms did much to give the administration of justice a genuine and much-needed immediacy, it was his work as a hands-on judge that left its most lasting and telling imprimatur on English law.

Mansfield's greatest forte was in the area of commercial or mercantile law. When he came to the bench, the common law was anchored in the customs and traditions of a very different – almost feudalistic – economy than was emerging in the mid-eighteenth century. His self-appointed task was to make the common law more facilitative of commercial activity in an increasingly global world. In the 1779 insurance case of *Milles v. Fletcher*, he made it plain that "the great object in every branch of the law, but especially in mercantile law, is certainty." His favored modus operandi was to draw on his wide learning in Roman law, Scottish law, and the French Code de Commerce. However, he did this in such a way that it reinvigorated the common law rather than replacing it with civilian elements; he wanted the common law to become the best it could be, not ape other systems of law for the sake of it. As he demonstrated in *Luke v. Lyde* in 1759, a maritime case about freight rates for lost goods, he refused to be hidebound by fixed rules and instead incorporated the changing customs and practice of trade and commerce. In a continuing series of cases throughout his tenure, he forged the basic building blocks of the law.

Mansfield also midwifed the law of insurance. Formulating it as a specialized region of contracts, he developed notions that still hold sway today. For example, in the 1766 case of *Carter v. Boehm*, the governor of Fort Marlborough (now Bengkulu on Sumatra, Indonesia) took out an insurance policy with Boehm against the chances and consequences of the fort being occupied by a foreign power. A Captain Tryon testified that, although Carter knew the fort was built to resist attacks from the local natives, it was not robust enough to withstand a likely assault by the French. When this occurred, Boehm reneged on his obligation to pay out under the policy. Mansfield sided with Governor Carter and held that he had acted with the required *uberrimae fides* (utmost good faith). In a judgment that could have been written yesterday, Mansfield argued that

> [i]nsurance is a contract based upon speculation. The special facts, upon which the contingent chance is to be computed, lie most commonly in the knowledge of the insured only; the underwriter trusts to his representation and proceeds upon the confidence that he does not keep back any circumstance in his knowledge, to mislead the underwriter into a belief that the circumstance does not exist, and to induce him to estimate the risk as if it did not exist. Good faith forbids either party by concealing what he privately knows, to draw the other into a bargain from his ignorance of that fact, and his believing the contrary.

One of Mansfield's particular innovations (which now looks a little suspect in intent and ambition) was his cultivation of a squad of jurymen. At a time when juries played a much more significant role in English private law, he selected a group of merchants to act as a special jury in commercial cases and ensured that they were appointed in important cases before him. Whereas he trained them in legal matters, they kept him informed of the best and most reputable practices in different areas of trade and commerce. As Lord Campbell put it, "he was on terms of the most familiar intercourse with them, not only conversing freely with them in Court, but inviting them to dine with him." Although this may seem a little contrived and improper today, it allowed Mansfield to make the common law into a living tradition, not simply an archaic body of ossified rules. Like most great judges, he did not let professional expectations get in the way of his efforts at necessary change.

However, not all of Mansfield's legal positions succeeded or stood the test of time. He tried to undermine the doctrine of consideration in contract law. Rather than requiring some exchange of value between the contracting parties, he urged a less rigid rule. In the 1765 case of *Pillans v. Van Mierop*, Mansfield held that a written promise in commercial settings was binding without more; it was the intention of the parties that was paramount. For him, the existence of consideration was to be an important evidentiary signal of a contract's legal bindingness, not its exclusive determinant. Although Mansfield continued to insist in the 1782 case of *Hawkes v. Saunders* that consideration could be implied from the existence of a moral obligation, this rule was reversed in a later 1840 case. Nevertheless, battle still rages among contract scholars and judges over the exact requirements of valid consideration. And Mansfield's views remain an assumed lightning rod in such engagements.

But Mansfield's contributions were not confined to commercial law. He did much to release the law of wills and estates from its medieval and highly formalistic origins. Consistent with his approach to contract law, he maintained that the controlling principle of construction should be the intention of the testator as understood by considering the whole of the testamentary document. In a telling anecdote, it is reported that, when confronted with a lawyer who was arguing that the testator's intentions should be understood in the context of the extensive body of precedents, Mansfield asked, "Sir, do you think that this old lady ever read those cases or would have understood them if she had?" As he stated more formally in the 1765 case of *Chapman v. Brown*, "the constant object of [construction] is to attain the intent; . . . implications shall supply verbal omissions; the letter shall give way; every inaccuracy of grammar, every impropriety of terms shall be corrected by the general meaning, if that be clear and manifest." However, occasionally his valor sometimes eclipsed his discretion. In the *Perrin v. Blake* case of 1770, his efforts to give the testator's intentions precedence over the accepted meaning of the technical phrases actually used was seen as a bridge too far by even those sympathetic to his general cause of bringing common sense to matters of legal interpretation.

Perhaps Mansfield's most memorable decision was in the slavery case of *Somerset v. Stewart* in 1772. The slave James Somerset was in England with his American owner, Charles Stewart. He attempted to flee from Stewart but was recaptured and imprisoned aboard the Jamaica-bound ship *Ann and Mary*. On behalf of Somerset, several abolitionists, including Granville Sharp, applied for a writ of habeas corpus (an order to produce a particular person) with respect to his imprisonment. At the time, although slavery was legal in America, it was not in England as such. After extensive hearings, Mansfield reserved and issued a brief two-hundred-word judgment. It was a bold pronouncement that brought together neatly many of the main themes in Mansfield's jurisprudence. Although he subtly avoided any grand or sweeping statements about the general legal status of slaves in England, he made it clear that their detainment in England was unlawful. Standing by his more general views on the superiority of the common law over legislation, he concluded that

> [t]he state of slavery is of such a nature, that it is incapable of now being introduced by Courts of Justice upon mere reasoning or inferences from any principles, natural or political; it must take its rise from positive law; the origin of it can in no country or age be traced back to any other source: immemorial usage preserves the memory of positive law long after all traces of the occasion; reason, authority, and time of its introduction are lost; and in a case so odious as the condition of slaves must be taken strictly, the power

claimed by this return was never in use here; no master ever was allowed here to take a slave by force to be sold abroad because he had deserted from his service, or for any other reason whatever; we cannot say the cause set forth by this return is allowed or approved of by the laws of this kingdom, therefore the man must be discharged.

This resounding judgment is rightly still considered to be one of the prized artifacts of English jurisprudence. Mindful that what was to become the United States was still an English colony, Mansfield managed in one fell swoop to banish almost all litigation about slavery from the English courts and to put great pressure on Parliament to abolish the slave trade. In his focused judgment, he undercut the moral legitimacy of slavery without mandating its legal abolition. For some, Mansfield's line treading was an insufficiently bold act of legal sophistry. But it ran firmly against the grain of elite opinion (which gained enormous economic benefits from the slave trade and its products) and helped to galvanize the political crusade for the total abolition of the slave trade. Sadly, it took another sixty years to bring about the complete emancipation of slaves in England in 1834.

Many gladly concur with historian Edward Foss's assessment of Mansfield as "the great oracle of the law" and that "there has never been a judge more venerated by his contemporaries, nor whose memory is regarded with greater respect and affection." However, that opinion was far from universal in Mansfield's day. A man of Mansfield's talents and accomplishments managed to generate more than his fair share of detractors over his long political and legal career. Indeed, Mansfield demonstrated that greatness is often not simply or even largely about keeping everyone happy, but about trying to do the right thing in the face of criticism. Popularity is sometimes a function, not a necessary feature, of greatness.

Apart from his numerous political opponents (including, of course, Pitt, who described him as "a very bad judge, proud, haughty to the Bar and hasty in his determinations"), Mansfield's strenuous and successful efforts to update the common law and the courts were guaranteed to stir up formidable opposition. He spent much of his career parrying efforts to expose his supposed Jacobite sympathies; this perhaps explains his failure to return to Scotland in light of the fact that his father and brother were both imprisoned for their Stuart allegiances and activities. But that same political experience had taught him some important skills in getting his own way and had given him a thick skin when it came to criticisms. In addition to his oratorical prowess, he also possessed great energy and a sense of administrative efficacy; his only recreational pursuit seemed to be horse riding. But there were several incidents in the latter parts of his career that place him in a less than flattering light.

In the years around 1770, a political critic (writing under the pseudonym Junius) began publishing letters that sought

Undated photograph of the monument at Lord Mansfield's tomb at Westminster Abbey, taken before 1912. The monument itself is the work of John Flaxman, and was erected at the north transept of the Abbey in 1801. *Source:* Courtesy of Historical & Special Collections, Harvard Law School Library.

to skewer the shenanigans of major political figures; Mansfield featured prominently in their number and was targeted for his Jacobite and more general Scottish connections as well as his continuing involvement in political matters while a judge. After one particular letter directed at King George III himself, Junius' publisher, Henry Woodfall, was charged with seditious libel. Even though Mansfield had been a target of Junius, he oversaw the trial and gave an uncompromising summing-up and direction to the jury that the words used amounted to libel as a matter of law. Yet, despite Mansfield's categorical charge, the jury found that Woodfall was "guilty of printing and publishing only," but not guilty of seditious libel. Mansfield was far from happy with this flagrant but unassailable challenge to his judicial authority; the fact that his rival Pitt supported the jury's decision only added to his bitterness. Nevertheless, Mansfield had enough sense to realize that further prosecutions were inadvisable. Instead, he recommended that the most effective course would be to ignore Junius and fail to rise to his unpalatable bait. Mansfield was proved right: Junius gave up his campaign a few months later in 1772.

In another incident, Mansfield became the direct object of dangerous public protests. As a result of the political upheaval around the Catholic Relief Bill of 1778 (which sought to emancipate Catholics from various civil and criminal impediments to full citizenship), large mobs roamed London. Allegedly spurred on by Lord George Gordon, a fellow Scot and Protestant politician, one particular group targeted Mansfield's house in Bloomsbury Square and burned it down; he was targeted as a defender of religious dissent. Although the mob seemed intent on hanging Mansfield, no one was seriously injured, but Mansfield lost all of his papers, manuscripts, and correspondence. Although he would not accept compensation for his losses, he did not let the matter go entirely – he presided over the treason trial of Lord Gordon. However, despite this colossal conflict of interest, Mansfield administered the short jury trial with professional equanimity. His summing-up was considered to be a model of balance and gave a full airing to the arguments and circumstances in support of Gordon's acquittal. As fate would have it, the jury returned a quick verdict of not guilty, because, although the riots were treasonable, there was insufficient evidence that Gordon had instigated or directed them. It was an outcome that seemed to vindicate both Gordon and Mansfield.

Although Mansfield is credited with coining (or, at least, reviving) the popular legal maxim *fiat justitia, ruat caelum* (let justice be done though the heavens fall), his own favorite was *boni judicis est ampliare justitiam* (the good judge's duty is to extend justice). Yet, as with so many other great figures, he is difficult to pigeonhole in his views on what constitutes an appropriate quality of justice. In the same way that his political affiliations seemed to cross the party lines of Whig and Tory and notwithstanding the historical context, his judicial philosophy often veered between liberal and conservative characterizations. Despite his condemnation of slavery, he remained largely unmoved by the brutality of the criminal process and its excessive sanctions. And for all his stands against religious persecution, he was a rabid opponent of the American colonies' efforts to gain independence. As one of his biographers, Bernard Shientag, summarized it, he was by and large "no noble humanitarian."

Yet, more than three centuries after his birth, Mansfield remains one of the few judges that garner widespread admiration and is thought of as the one English judge who stands head and shoulders above both his contemporaries and many of those that came later. As the famous early nineteenth-century American scholar and judge Joseph Story concluded (along with Julian Waterman), Mansfield "'broke down the narrow barrier of the common law' and redeemed it from 'feudal selfishness and barbarity,'" and "he was one of those great men raised up by Providence, at a fortunate moment, to effect a salutary revolution in the world." It is a measure of that revolution's significance that its effects are still being felt today. Lord Mansfield was a great judge not only because of what he did (and he did plenty), but also because of the pioneering example that he set of what might be done. He showed that judges could, with determination and vision, make the common law into its own "fountain of justice." Although it might never "work itself pure," common law could constantly work itself more just and, in doing so, better serve society and its changing demands.

When Mansfield retired from the bench on 4 June 1788, he was eighty-three years old. By the standards of his time, he was a very old man and had outlived most of his contemporaries and rivals; his wife, Elizabeth, had died in April 1784. Nevertheless, he had been reluctant to retire. He was concerned that William Pitt, the son of Mansfield's lifelong rival and then the twenty-nine-year old prime minister, would fail to appoint the loyal and deserving Francis Buller as his successor as Lord Chief Justice. In a final act of Pittish one-upmanship, Buller was overlooked and Lloyd Kenyon was appointed to the prestigious judicial post. Although he was not in the best of health, Mansfield lived for another five years. He spent most of his time at his home, Kenwood House in Hampstead Heath, and pottered around in his beloved gardens; he was still riding into his seventies. He died on 20 March 1793 and was duly buried in the North Cross at Westminster Abbey along with other luminaries of the age. Lincoln's Inn still offers a series of scholarships for aspiring barristers in Lord Mansfield's name.

When the young Murray rode south from Scotland in 1718, he surely could not have anticipated that he would be commencing a journey that would take him to the very summit of the English political and legal establishment. His achievements and lasting fame are impressive by any standards, let alone by those of a "foreigner." To be a Scotsman in eighteenth-century England was to court suspicion and often resentment. Yet he not only overcame such obstacles but also did so in a style and with a degree of success that is the best testimony to his talents. When it suited him, he made much of his outsider status and leveraged it to his and others' advantage. In transforming himself from the lovelorn and impecunious young William Murray to the respected and powerful Earl of Mansfield, he also changed the common law and courts in a way that few others have been able to equal since. In the process, he set the bar very high for those later judges who aspired to judicial greatness. There are few contemporaries of his, let alone judges, who can lay claim centuries later to almost equal and lasting appeal as his friend, the poetic and still relevant Alexander Pope.

3

John Marshall

A Founding Judge

I t is difficult to reduce the qualities of greatness to any simple social equation or historical formula. However, there are some coefficients that offer a reliable guide – talent, opportunity, force of personality, vision, and timing. Although many possess some of these qualities, it is only a small few who are fortunate to have them all and who are also able to combine them in an authentic and winning manner. In the more confined world of judges, these same attributes can mark certain individuals as members of a distinct elite. Although a number of judges are considered great in their time, it is only a handful whose reputation can persist and perhaps grow as the decades pass by. History has a way of confounding as much as confirming both the identity of great judges and the standards for identifying them.

One of those judges who can lay a relatively uncontroversial claim to greatness is the American John Marshall from the early nineteenth century. His is a rags-to-riches or, more accurately, cabin-to-chiefship story with lots of remarkable accommodations in between. He played a central and multifaceted role in the founding of the United States as the constitutional democracy it is today. His influence as first a politician and then more prominently a judge is second to none; it has shaped the role and performance of judges for more than two hundred years. Although there is little debate about him being included in the undisputed cast of great judges that have dominated the common law tradition, there is still much to discuss about exactly what qualities he possessed that have recommended him to so many as the quintessential great judge. If all the reports are true, John Marshall was one of those who demonstrated that nice guys really can finish first.

John Marshall was born on 24 September 1755 to Thomas and Mary (Isham Keith) Marshall. He was to be the eldest of fifteen siblings, with eight sisters and six brothers. Born in a log cabin deep in the northwest woods of Virginia near Germantown (now Midland) in a roadside village in the frontier county of Fauquier, John was to become a legendary American who ushered in and bridged the important historical gap between colonial government and constitutional independence. He stands with his contemporaries, like George Washington and Thomas Jefferson, as a deserving leader of a storied generation.

The Marshall family was part of the original pioneering stock that had come over from the United Kingdom in the early seventeenth century. On John's father's side, his ancestors were from a slave-owning background and, after emigrating from Wales, had made a living working second-rate land that had been abandoned by more wealthy families, like the Washingtons and Popes. His mother's side had loose connections to the English gentry, and although there were some lawyers and academics among their number, they were largely soldiers. A shared characteristic was that the Marshalls and the Keiths were prolific in the number of offspring produced, even by the standards of the time.

Thomas Marshall had received a bare education but was determined that his own children would receive much better opportunities than he had. Working as a land agent (surveying and maintaining land as well as collecting rents), he was fortunate in that his employer, Lord Fairfax, was a generous and progressive man. He encouraged Thomas to better himself. Thomas duly obliged by becoming Fauquier County's first magistrate, and he was elected to the representative House of Burgesses in 1761. As a politician, he played a prominent role in encouraging his fellow colonists to resist unpopular British rule and achieved the rank of colonel in the War of Independence in the late 1770s. Incidentally, it was Lord Mansfield (see Chapter 2) who was lined up on the other side as an implacable opponent of American independence.

John was the beneficiary of his father's ambitions for him, Lord Fairfax's generosity in giving access to his extensive library, and his mother's intelligence and steady temperament. Growing up in increasingly better houses built by his father's own hands and efforts, young John had all the privileges and burdens of being the oldest in his large family; he spent a large part of his time hunting, fishing, and caring for his siblings. But, like all his brothers and also sisters (which was relatively rare at the time), he was expected to pursue his educational studies under the tutelage of his father, who he came to regard as "both a watchful parent and an affectionate friend." John was a gifted student and developed a particular affection for English literature. However, his father recognized that John needed more guidance, so, at fourteen, he was sent away to Washington's Campbell Academy. After a year there, he returned home to be tutored by the local Scottish minister, James Thomson, who introduced John to Latin and Greek. At this time, he was also reading Blackstone's recently published *Commentaries on the Laws of England*, which his father had purchased as part of his plan to steer John toward a career in law.

By then, the Marshalls had become a family of greater substance and standing. John's father had acquired a 1,700-acre estate at North Cobbler Mountain; this was near the village of Salem, which was later to be renamed after the Marshalls. At the age of seventeen, John helped build Oak

Lithograph of John Marshall in profile, created 1888. *Source:* Courtesy of Historical & Special Collections, Harvard Law School Library.

Hill, his family's seven-room frame house. Although it was far from being a mansion-like estate in the style of the Madisons or Jeffersons, it remained a favored retreat for John throughout his life; he visited there to escape from his more pressured and official life in Richmond and Washington, DC. He became its owner in 1785 after his parents moved to Kentucky.

When the War of Independence began in 1775, the twenty-year-old John enlisted. After a spell in the local

Culpeper Minutemen, he was commissioned as a first lieutenant in the Fauquier Rifles. From there, he followed his father and his own patriotic instincts to join Washington's army in New York. After seeing considerable action (including the Battle of Stoney Point in June 1779), he returned to Virginia and gave up his captaincy. Unlike Holmes (see Chapter 4), Marshall seemed to carry no lasting psychological damage from his battlefield action. Having fulfilled his military and communal responsibilities, he began what was to become his main career and lasting vocation – he enrolled in law school in May 1780.

John was one of the first students to complete the legal curriculum prescribed by Chancellor George Wythe at the College of William and Mary in Williamsburg. The course only lasted for a few short and intensive but very formative weeks. Along with his eighty classmates, he studied the works of the political Montesquieu, the philosophical Hume, and especially the legal Blackstone, with whom he was already on very familiar terms. He was a serious and gifted student who joined the elite Phi Beta Kappa fraternity, where he met future Supreme Court colleague Bushrod Washington, George's nephew, and a leading Virginia judge, Spencer Roane, who was to be one of his principal judicial antagonists over federal power and the authority of the Supreme Court. On 28 August 1780, John obtained his license to practice law; it was signed by Governor Thomas Jefferson, a man with whom Marshall would engage in a lifelong rivalry.

While a law student, John became entranced by a woman named Polly Ambler; he scribbled her name throughout the margins of his notebooks. Born Mary Willis Ambler, she was the daughter of Thomas Jefferson's first lover, Rebecca Burwell, who had married a wealthy Virginia businessman, Jacqulin Ambler. Although John and Polly's early meetings were not auspicious, the rustic John fell for the more polished Polly. In pursuing her, he became the "very hurricane of a lover." After a fervent courtship, the couple was married on 3 January 1783. The twenty-seven-year-old John and sixteen-year-old Polly were blessed with a close marriage; they not only remained together for forty-nine years, until her death on Christmas Day 1831, but they did so with considerable happiness. Spending most of their time in Richmond, they had ten children, of which only six lived to adulthood. The eldest, Thomas, emerged as a leader in the struggle to end slavery in Virginia. Sadly, Polly's later years were plagued by ill health and depression. It was a credit to John that he was an attentive and concerned partner who pitched in, along with the servants, to care for Polly and to fill many household duties.

After a short period in private practice in Fauquier County, John followed his father into politics. He was elected to the Virginia House of Delegates, where he served until 1789 (and again from 1795 to 1796); he sided with those who advocated a general government strong enough to ensure public safety. Although he was not enamored of legislative politics, he was voted at the age of twenty-seven onto the

Council of State (a cabinet-like executive body that was charged with the day-to-day administration of Virginia). It was there that he developed his deep commitment to the idea that constitutions had supremacy and must be recognized as so being. In a heated controversy over whether the legislature could discipline magistrates, Marshall held firm to the principle that the constitutional separation of powers prevented the legislative branch from riding roughshod over the judicial branch. In 1785, he also obtained the position of recorder for the city of Richmond that gave him his first experience as a judge.

In June 1788, Marshall was selected as a delegate to the Virginia Convention, which was charged with ratifying or rejecting the proposed U.S. Constitution. This was a coveted position, and it promoted Marshall to the elevated company of the Founding Fathers. He did not take center stage but was a firm and consistent advocate with James Madison and others on behalf of ratification; his contribution covers nine tightly argued pages of the closely printed official record of the debates. Not unexpectedly, he saved his most forceful interventions for the debate on the power of the judiciary. According to Marshall (and in opposition to Jefferson), the strengthening of the judiciary was a much-needed improvement. In a speech that presaged his later judicial utterances, he said that

[i]s it not necessary that the federal courts should have cognizance of cases arising under the constitution, and the

laws of the United States? What is the Service or purpose of a judiciary, but to execute the laws in a peaceable, orderly manner, without shedding blood, or creating a contest, or availing yourselves of force? If this be the case, where can its jurisdiction be more necessary than here? To what quarter will you look for protection from an infringement on the constitution, if you will not give the power to the judiciary?

After playing his part in ensuring that the Constitution was ratified, Marshall retired from the Virginia legislature. Although he was heavily courted by Madison and his Federalist supporters to run for the federal House of Representatives, Marshall declined. Furthermore, although he was approved by the Senate as U.S. attorney for Virginia in September 1789, he also passed on this opportunity. Although he would have liked the post, he sensed the demands imposed on him would have forced him to cut back on his blossoming law practice in Richmond. Indeed, throughout his political career, Marshall had continued to work as a lawyer. He was known less for his oratorical skills than for his argumentative skills; he was very effective at rebutting others' submissions and specialized in appellate work. By the late 1780s, he was a leading member of the Richmond bar. Although he concentrated on property cases, he also had success in other areas of law. In *Bracken v. William and Mary College* in 1790, he persuaded the court that his client, the prestigious school, was not a public entity but "a private eleemosynary institution" governed entirely by its own board of visitors. Also, in the 1786 case of *Hite v. Fairfax*, he argued on behalf of his old aristocratic mentor in an important case about prior rights in land ownership.

In May 1797, Marshall was prevailed on by President John Adams to act, along with Charles Cotesworth Pinckney and Elbridge Gerry, as a special envoy to France. The French had been engaged in a belligerent series of maritime acts against the United States and its vital commercial interests. He was disinclined to become involved, but his sense of patriotic duty got the better of him. After engaging in a productive diplomatic mission, he was successful in bringing hostilities to an end and curtailing the maneuvers of French buccaneers. For his troubles, he was feted by both houses of Congress. Ironically, this had the effect of making the reluctant Marshall even more in demand on the federal scene.

For a while, Marshall resisted the entreaties from Washington, DC. He declined the offer of a seat in the cabinet as attorney general and even turned aside an appointment to the Supreme Court bench; his former student classmate, Bushrod Washington, took the vacancy. However, he was beginning to relent. In the spring of 1799, he agreed to become a candidate for Congress. Despite concerted and fierce opposition, Marshall was elected by a small majority. He took his seat on 4 March 1799. His short tenure was marked by regular and measured speeches from the floor; he was admired by his colleagues for his experience as well as judgment in public affairs. When Congress adjourned in May 1800, Marshall finally accepted President Adams's invitation to take a seat in the reorganized cabinet. Consequently, he became secretary of state on 6 June 1800 and resigned his seat in Congress. As the president spent the summer in Massachusetts, he assumed the role of chief executive; he used this opportunity to improve further the U.S. relationship with France.

Once Marshall was a key part of the Washington power elite, President Adams came knocking again. In his last month of office in January 1801, he offered Marshall the position of Chief Justice of the United States; this broke with the tradition of offering it to a sitting member. This time, Marshall accepted, and he was installed on 4 February 1801. In an odd decision for someone who was so committed to the constitutional separation of powers, he continued as secretary of state for another month, until his successor was appointed. At his oath taking, the democratic Marshall insisted on wearing a plain black robe rather than the traditional ermine-trimmed scarlet. At forty-five, John Marshall was to be only the fourth Chief Justice of the United States and went on to serve for a still record-setting term of thirty-five years, under five presidents (Jefferson, Madison, James Monroe, John Quincy Adams, and Andrew Jackson). Adams later wrote that "the proudest act of my life was the gift of John Marshall to the people of the United States."

Marshall's predecessors as Chief Justice had left little lasting impression on the work and jurisprudence of the

Supreme Court. Indeed, on Marshall's arrival, the court played a much more limited and lesser role in the governance of the United States than either the executive or legislative branches. Indeed, even among courts, the Supreme Court was considered less powerful than leading state courts. It was to be his chosen task to push the court more deeply into the heart of America's constitutional and political operations. As one commentator concluded, Marshall "transformed the Constitution from a compact among the states into a charter of national life." In so doing, he secured for himself as well as the Supreme Court a preeminent position in the country's evolution. Although he has much to answer for in effecting this controversial and seismic change, both supporters and detractors alike can agree that American law and judging would never be the same again. John Marshall initiated a mode of judicial review whose contours and constraints are still being redrawn and debated today.

At an institutional level, Marshall made significant changes. He sought to introduce a more convivial esprit de corps among the judges. For instance, he organized things so that the justices would live together in the same hotel or boarding house whenever the court convened and encouraged a more respectable court demeanor. Nevertheless, on rainy days, the judges would enliven their conferences with wine. Even when the sun was shining, Marshall would order wine anyway, because he noted that "our jurisdiction is so vast that it might be raining somewhere." More tellingly, he got rid of the lingering English practice of each judge delivering separate opinions; this was to give the opinions of the court more gravity and legitimacy. Often, this opinion would be delivered by Marshall himself as Chief Justice to further consolidate the court's standing. This was a practice that Jefferson, the major opponent of the Federalists, railed against at every political opportunity.

In the early years of Marshall's chiefship, the Supreme Court had six members. More significantly, they all tended to take a broadly Federalist stance in which the power of federal government was seen to be more important than that of the states; there were almost no dissents delivered. However, in 1805, new appointees resisted the Federalist orthodoxy and began to display a more republican sensibility; dissenting opinions became more common. This division of opinion among the judges accelerated with the increase in membership to seven in 1807 (and then nine in 1837). By 1812, the court had stabilized, and the same seven judges continued for twelve successive years. During this period, Marshall (along with Joseph Story, Bushrod Washington, and ofttimes Gabriel Duvall) managed to exercise strong administrative, intellectual, and political leadership. After 1824, this controlling coalition began to exert less influence, and the court was less predictable or consistent in its rulings. However, in addition to writing almost half of the court's opinions, it is notable that Marshall only wrote dissenting opinions in eight of the more than 1,100 opinions delivered between 1801 and 1835; this is far fewer than any chief justice since.

However, there can be no doubt that it is Marshall's contribution to the constitutional position of the courts and their development of substantive legal doctrine that most stands out. His accomplishments in this regard are truly and deservedly legendary. Over his long tenure as chief justice, he made many contributions to American jurisprudence and life. In cases like *Fletcher v. Peck* in 1810, *Trustees of Dartmouth College v. Woodward* in 1819, and *Gibbons v. Ogden* in 1824, he also laid much of the foundations for the development of a more modern economy that protected commerce and corporations; he has been celebrated and criticized for these important efforts to put the capitalist economy on a more secure and privileged footing. In the field of international law, he consolidated legal doctrines that demanded strict fidelity to treaties, reciprocal recognition of other governments' sovereignty, and advancement of appropriate frameworks for free trade. While doing all this, he also found time to research and write a five-volume biography, titled *The Life of Washington*, which was published in 1807; it was also praised and panned for its Federalist leanings.

But Marshall's effects on the architecture and dynamics of the broader constitutional system are his most memorable and defining contributions. Over his tenure, he established principles that now are considered axiomatic to the functioning of the American Constitution. From 1801 to 1835, the Supreme Court's role went through a marked metamorphosis from institutional bit player to constitutional mainstay. The sweep and ambition of Marshall's work are most ably

Portrait of John Marshall by Henry Inman, 1832. *Source:* Public domain.

showcased in the heralded decisions of *Marbury* and *Mc-Culloch*; they are the raw materials of both Marshall's claim to greatness and the continuing structure of the American constitutional order.

Although the facts of *Marbury v. Madison* are somewhat technical and obscure, the import of the judgment is profound and far reaching. In addition to appointing Marshall late in his term of office, President Adams had also appointed William Marbury as a justice of the peace for the District of Columbia. Although confirmed by the Senate and signed by the president, Marbury's commission had not been delivered when Jefferson succeeded to the presidency. When the new president refused to deliver the commission, Marbury sought an order from the Supreme Court to mandate its delivery by the secretary of state, James Madison; Marbury contended that the Judiciary Act of 1789 had authorized the court to issue so-called writs of mandamus (an enforcement order) in appropriate cases like his own. The strict legal issue was whether Marbury had a right to the commission and, if so, what legal remedy was available to him. However, the underlying and more important issue was the meaning and effect of the Constitution and who had the power to determine that, Congress or the Supreme Court.

Writing for the court, Marshall decided that, although Marbury did have a valid claim under the Judiciary Act, the 1789 act was unconstitutional, and, therefore, the court did not possess the power to enforce Marbury's judicial commission. Article III of the Constitution, which laid out the Supreme Court's jurisdiction, was at the heart of the matter. Whereas Marbury argued that the Constitution established a floor only for the courts' jurisdiction and that Congress could add to it, the Supreme Court determined that Congress had no such power to modify the Supreme Court's jurisdiction. In reaching this conclusion, Marshall went out of his way to announce that it is the Supreme Court, not Congress or the executive branch, that had the ultimate authority to determine the meaning of the Constitution and whether or not legislation or government action was constitutional. In his famous words, Marshall left no doubt in people's minds about the proper fulcrum of constitutional authority:

> So, if a law be in opposition to the Constitution, if both the law and the Constitution apply to a particular case, so that the Court must either decide that case conformably to the law, disregarding the Constitution, or conformably to the Constitution, disregarding the law, the Court must determine which of these conflicting rules governs the case. This is of the very essence of judicial duty.

> If, then, the Courts are to regard the Constitution, and the Constitution is superior to any ordinary act of the Legislature, the Constitution, and not such ordinary act, must govern the case to which they both apply.

> Those, then, who controvert the principle that the Constitution is to be considered in court as a paramount law are reduced to the necessity of maintaining that courts must close their eyes on the Constitution, and see only the law.

> This doctrine would subvert the very foundation of all written Constitutions. It would declare that an act which, according to the principles and theory of our government, is entirely void, is yet, in practice, completely obligatory. It would declare that, if the Legislature shall do what is expressly forbidden, such act, notwithstanding the express prohibition, is in reality effectual. It would be giving to the

Legislature a practical and real omnipotence with the same breath which professes to restrict their powers within narrow limits. It is prescribing limits, and declaring that those limits may be passed at pleasure.

Needless to say, this stance did not go down well with President Jefferson and other Republican-minded politicians. Indeed, the contemporary significance of Marshall's judgment was more political than legal; it can be read as a cautionary lecture by the Federalist Marshall to the Republican Jefferson on the Rule of Law's primacy over politics – no person or institution (not even the president or Congress) can claim to be superior to or beyond the Constitution. The fact that Marshall was still the acting secretary of state at the time Marbury's commission was supposed to be initially delivered can be seen to undercut the principled (as opposed to the politically expedient) nature of his decision.

However, the lasting importance of Marshall's *Marbury* judgment is to be found in its affirmation of the Supreme Court's authoritative practice of judicial review and its effect of putting the Supreme Court front and center in the dramatic scheme of constitutional politics. Marshall enabled the court to assert itself against the executive branch without declaring the specific legislation unconstitutional and, therefore, without taking the risk that an unenforceable remedy against the executive branch would simply be ignored. With this very canny piece of political maneuvering, he asserted institutional authority against both coordinate branches of government but minimized the confrontation in doing so.

Although there was some historical and legal precedent for Marshall's position, it was a bold and decisive move. Although the decision made a sharp distinction between matters of law (for the courts) and politics (for the legislature and executive), it was clear that the vital power to determine the location and extent of these separate zones was vested in the Supreme Court. Even though Marshall's reasoning – "questions, in their nature political . . . can never be made in this court" – was far from overwhelming in scope or force, it managed to carry the day as well as posterity. Judicial review is now viewed by many as an indispensable and inevitable corollary of a written constitution. Ironically, after establishing the power, Marshall himself never again exercised it in holding that an act of Congress or of a president was unconstitutional; it was a half century later, in the notorious case of *Dred Scott*, before the invalidating power was used.

Today, the worth of Marshall's entrenchment of judicial review is still, of course, hotly debated. A vocal minority holds that judicial review is neither indispensable nor inevitable. It is argued that it is possible (and more desirable) in a democracy to develop other methods and sites through which to safeguard and implement a constitution; there is no magic or particular merit to having unelected judges determine controversial issues. However, although a majority of commentators defend the legitimacy of judicial review, they are very much at odds over how judges should go about fulfilling this enormous responsibility. Recognizing the constant threat of what Jefferson termed "the despotism of an oligarchy," debate tends to be joined over the approach that judges should take to interpreting and enforcing the Constitution.

Despite the power of his central idea, Marshall seemed more than a little naïve in his understanding of how his judicial successors might exercise this potentially awesome power. This is especially so when it is remembered that the Constitution must be able to apply to later societies that bear little resemblance to that of Marshall and his fellow founders. Few cases come before the courts that do not offer competing yet plausible interpretations of the Constitution – how are the judges to decide between them? What is the methodological basis of judicial review? Does the Constitution really have a meaning that is more than the sum total of the sitting justices' opinions? As Marshall himself noted, there must be a workable distinction between law and politics. But he did not appreciate that there seems to be no obvious or uncontroversial way to draw that distinction that is not itself political or open ended.

Some of these challenges to the wisdom of Marshall's *Marbury* judgment can be glimpsed in his equally renowned 1819 decision of *McCulloch v. The State of Maryland*. Amid a raging national debate, the state of Maryland imposed a tax on all out-of-state banks. However, as the federal

Second Bank of the United States was the only one operating in Maryland, the tax was clearly aimed at hampering the bank's operation. When the bank's manager, James McCulloch, refused to pay the tax, the Maryland government commenced legal proceedings. One of Maryland's contentions was that, as the Constitution made no mention of any federal power to charter banks, the Second Bank had no constitutional status. The federal government argued that its powers were not limited to those explicitly provided for in the Constitution's list of express powers, provided the laws enacted are in useful furtherance of Congress's given powers under the Constitution.

Relying on the "necessary and proper" clause, Marshall delivered a unanimous opinion for the Supreme Court only twelve days after the hearing. He held that, although there was no express power to incorporate banks, the act to set up the Second Bank was within the constitutional authority of the federal government; the federal government's express powers are supplemented by certain implied powers. In a ringing endorsement of the supremacy of national interests, Marshall stated that

> [a]lthough among the enumerated powers of government we do not find the word Bank, or Incorporation, we find the great powers to lay and collect taxes, to borrow money, to regulate commerce, to declare and conduct a war, and to raise and support armies and navies.... The government, which has a right to do an act, and has imposed on it the duty of performing that act, must, according to the dictates

of reason, be allowed to select the means; and those who contend that it may not select any appropriate means, that one particular mode of effecting the objective is excepted, take upon themselves to prove the exception. . . . To employ the means necessary to an end is generally understood as employing any means calculated to produce the end, and not as being confined to those single means without which the end would be entirely unattainable. . . .

We admit, as all must admit that the powers of government are limited, and that its limits are not to be transcended. But we think the sound construction of the Constitution must allow to the national legislature that discretion, with respect to the means by which the powers it confers are to be carried into execution, which will enable that body to perform the high duties assigned to it, in the manner most beneficial to the people. Let the end be legitimate, let it be within the scope of the Constitution, and all means which are appropriate, which are plainly adapted to that end, which are not prohibited, but consist with the letter and spirit of the Constitution, are constitutional.

This decision granted enormous power to the federal government and conclusively determined that state action cannot curtail the valid exercise of federal authority. It was a massive victory for the Federalist forces and tilted the political playing field decisively in their favor. Apart from that, Marshall's judgment also gives the lie to the idea that the Constitution is simply one more piece of legislation to be interpreted by courts. As the country's supreme law, it was considered to deserve a more expansive and sensitive treatment; he was insistent that it was the archprinciple of "popular sovereignty" that anchored the decision. As he famously uttered in *McCulloch*, "we must never forget that it is *a Constitution* we are expounding." This somewhat enigmatic statement has become talismanic in the world of constitutional interpretation; it is called in aid by almost everyone to justify their own take on the special duty of fixing constitutional meaning. Even though the political battle over states' rights continues today, it takes place within the capacious shadow of Marshall's epochal judgment in *McCulloch*.

In the early 1970s, a couple of legal scholars did a survey to appraise the relative performances of all the justices who had sat on the Supreme Court. They consulted sixty-five law school deans and professors of law, history, and political science who taught or wrote in the field of constitutional law. There was only one justice who was unanimously chosen as deserving the rating of "great" – John Marshall. There is no reason to argue with such a rare consensus. But it does afford an opportunity to isolate the qualities that might be considered to be associated with his agreed greatness.

The fact that John Marshall was a well-loved and simple man was integral to his success and reputation as a judge and public figure. A committed Protestant churchgoer, he sought to lead a virtuous and dignified life; he had a sense of humor and enjoyed the company of others. Lacking airs

Photograph of Richmond, Virginia home of Chief Justice John Marshall, c. 1905. *Source:* Library of Congress - Prints and Photographs Division [LC-D4-18410].

and graces, he was a modest man who seemed to be not only respected but also liked by most people with whom he came in contact. As one biographer summarized, "no American citizen except Washington ever conciliated so large a measure of popularity and public esteem." Beginning with his role as an older brother to his fourteen siblings, he assumed the responsibilities of leadership with a natural ease. The quality of being able to pull people around to his viewpoint and to win personal and intellectual loyalty was instrumental in his work as chief justice. It should not be forgotten that many of his most important and influential judgments, like *Marbury* and *McCulloch*, were unanimous; Marshall had the advantage of being able to speak with the weighty authority of a full court behind him. Consequently, his ability to forge such alliances without deviating from his vision of what was best for the new American republic cannot be underestimated in assessing his greatness.

Marshall was a great judge in spite of, not because of, his writing style. As his leading judgments attest, he was not blessed with the gifts of literary fluency; he did not have the apothegmatic knack of Lord Mansfield (see Chapter 2). Although his judgments read clearly and simply, they do not possess the rhetorical flourish of those of Holmes (see Chapter 4) or even Benjamin Cardozo. But they served their purpose and, at a time when Supreme Court judgments were more broadly read than today (at least by the social and political elite), his straightforward style connected well with his audience. Preferring function over form, Marshall cut and styled his legal cloth to suit the wearers' needs. Indeed, it is a telling indication of his greatness that he managed to impose and have accepted his Federalist vision of the American polity at a time when its merit and appeal were far from widespread or uncontested. In achieving this, he was able to rely on the political capital that he had accumulated over the years as a man of integrity and standing. Of course, it did not harm him that he was able to draw on the moral clout of his revered status as a Founding Father. With acuity and craft, Marshall was able to pull off the considerable trick of converting his political prowess into legal authority.

At the root of all Marshall's political skills and legal talents was his sense of judgment and common sense. Although he was a reluctant celebrity, he did not allow his personal reservations to eclipse his civic devotion. He was courted by others for his genuine capacity to grasp the nub of any problem and to offer solutions that would then seem almost obvious to others who had previously been befuddled as to what to do. This facility to combine abstract book learning with earthy life lessons served him equally well in both his political and judicial life. Accordingly, Marshall persuaded and impressed others with his time-honed instincts for making the right decision at the right time in the right way. As such, he was that rare figure who blended principle and pragmatism as well as subtlety and substance into a paradoxical but appealing jurisprudential project that won over his peers and has withstood the test of time.

Like others before and after him, Chief Justice John Marshall respected the idea and ideals of law at the same time as he worked to overhaul them. But, in his commitment to the Rule of Law, he did not feel compelled to conform to its existing shape and substance; he was willing to rework it in line with a more compelling and capacious understanding of what he believed was required in a burgeoning constitutional democracy. Of course, it helped that he was writing on a relatively blank slate; the Supreme Court had not yet staked out any distinctive constitutional role for itself in the early decades of the nineteenth century. Nevertheless, it took a judge of special abilities and, as importantly, an innovative appreciation of what new kind of judging was needed to meet the exigencies of the time. Although his chosen path of an active and involved judiciary was not (and still is not) to all Democrats' liking, Marshall transformed the role of the judge as he strived to fulfill its institutional demands. In this way, he was a new game maker as much as an old game changer.

Like other impressive figures of history, John Marshall had the gift of opportune timing. His personal attributes and political nous were ideally suited to the challenge that faced his society and nation at a particular juncture in history. At another time, his particular gifts might have been ill matched to the contours of contemporary challenges. But, even as he set a course that often went against the currents of popular opinion, he was attuned to the perceived needs of his society. He had the wherewithal and moxie to follow his civic and constitutional intuitions; his training in both the philosophical canon at William and Mary and the political trenches of the nation's founding was not lost on him. He was an uncommon man with a common touch. As Oliver Wendell Holmes Jr., another titan of the American judicial scene (see Chapter 4), noted, "if American law were to be represented by a single figure, sceptic and worshipper alike would agree that the figure could be one alone, and that one, John Marshall." He was the block off which other judicial chips would gratefully fall.

Unlike today, being a Supreme Court justice was not an all-consuming undertaking in the early decades of the nineteenth century. Marshall spent the bulk of his time in Richmond with his family. He was 100 miles away in Washington, DC, for about three months when the court was in session and about 150 miles away for several weeks when he would sit on the circuit court in Raleigh, North Carolina. This gave him time to do much else. He was active in local Richmond politics and, in 1829, became again a delegate to the state constitutional convention, at which he was reunited with his old allies, James Madison and James Munroe. Although he had been a slave owner, he was the first president of the Richmond branch of the American Colonization Society, which sought to resettle slaves in Liberia, West Africa. Also, his completion of a serious and substantial biography of Washington added to his active and fulfilling civic life.

In the spring of 1831, after serving for an energetic thirty years as chief justice, the seventy-six-year-old Marshall's health began to fail. He was diagnosed with bladder stones. Later in the year, he underwent a successful operation in Philadelphia. But, returning to Richmond, he found his beloved Polly in critical condition. John stayed at her side for the next week, but to no avail. Polly died on Christmas Day 1831. The day before she died, she removed her locket that contained a strand of hair from the courting years; John wore the locket for the rest of his life. After her death, John was never quite the same; he had lost the spring in his step. Yet he soldiered on and continued to fulfill his judicial duties. However, in early summer 1835, he fell victim to liver disease. He died in Philadelphia at the age of eighty on the evening of 6 July 1835; his son Thomas had been struck by lighting and died a week earlier, but John had been spared that news. In accordance with his wishes, he received a modest funeral and was buried next to Polly in Shockoe Hill Cemetery in Richmond. He had lived to be the second-last surviving Founding Father.

John Marshall is remembered not only as one of the undisputed great judges but also as a true hero of the American tradition. He received many honors during his lifetime, including degrees from Harvard and Princeton. Since then, his life has been commemorated in so many ways – his Richmond home is a heritage site; there is a large statue of him in the Supreme Court building; he featured as the face of treasury notes in 1890; and there was a forty-cent stamp issued in his honor on his two-hundredth birthday in September 1955. But perhaps the most fitting tribute came from his own hand. Two days before he died, he penned his own epitaph. Its simplicity and humility somehow resounds in perfect counterpoint to his immense life and national contribution:

John Marshall
son of Thomas and Mary Marshall
was born on the 24th of September 1755
Intermarried with Mary Willis Ambler
the 3rd of January 1783
Departed this life
the sixth day of July 1835.

4

Oliver Wendell Holmes Jr.

The Magnificent Yankee

Great figures have a tendency to polarize popular opinion. Acting as lightning rods for controversy, these characters hold strong opinions and express them forcefully. Their views and actions touch a nerve in the popular consciousness and galvanize both approval and disapproval. In many ways that is why they are great; this characteristic speaks as much to the intensity of their sway as it does to their merit. They manage to occupy a position that stands on the fringes of received views but strikes at the heart of the times. Sometimes unappreciated in their own lifetimes and occasionally vilified, their influence casts a long shadow and is the stuff of debate for many years to come.

Oliver Wendell Holmes is one of those figures. It is no exaggeration to say that this magnificent Yankee stands as a colossus astride the American legal system and still manages to exert a strong pull on today's judging and its theoretical basis generally. With his imposing demeanor and his enviable ability to turn a phrase, he is that rare entity whose legacy can be challenged but not ignored. He possessed a capacity to crystallize sharply the emerging viewpoints on a topic and to shape them into a new way of thinking. He was not only a fund of penetrating questions but also a resource of provocative answers. Over his long and varied career, he became an iconic presence on the academic and judicial scene. Few others can claim to have made such an impression, both good and bad, on the minds of lawyers and jurists. He is the law's Jekyll and Hyde.

Oliver Wendell Holmes Jr. was a true American blue blood. A scion of one of the upper-crust families who made up the Boston Brahmins, his life and career spanned the transformative century from the colonial 1840s to the industrialized 1930s. From an early age, he rubbed shoulders with some of the great-and-good of American society and was destined to swell its ranks. He shouldered great expectations and fulfilled them in the most compelling manner. It seemed that it was never a question of whether "Wendy" would do something suitably important and influential, but only a question of what precisely that contribution would be. From his soldierly service in the Civil War through to his judicial performance during the Great Depression, Holmes left a mark on American law and letters that remains as unique as it is contested.

On 8 March 1841, Oliver entered the world in Cambridge, Massachusetts, as the elder son of Amelia Lee and Oliver Wendell Holmes. He was known as "Junior" to his more senior father, both as a matter of genealogy and also, at least from the young Oliver's standpoint, achievement. The Holmes family's pedigree was impeccable. Connected through intermarriage and social status to anyone who was anyone in polite and elite Boston society, Oliver's collection of relatives was studded with judges, theologians, scholars, and literary figures. His father was a doctor by training. Even though he became dean of Harvard Medical School, he earned his lasting fame as a poet and novelist. When he was twenty-one, he wrote the patriotic "Old Ironsides," which garnered national attention and solidified his growing reputation. He went on to write many essays and books, of which the most well known is *The Autocrat of the Breakfast Table* in 1858. He was a demanding father and a very hard act to follow; their relationship was always strained and straining.

From an early age, the young Wendy was simply expected to excel and burnish the family's standing. As a child of privilege, he was surrounded by the Boston intelligentsia and summered as a youth with, among others, Nathaniel Hawthorne and Henry Wadsworth Longfellow. It was a privileged upbringing and also a pressured one. He turned for emotional support to his mother, but also to his Uncle John and family friend Ralph Waldo Emerson, with whom he shared a close relationship. Nevertheless, he was no great prodigy at school and, by the elevated standards of his immediate circle, made no great impression. This continued in his undergraduate days at the local Harvard University. It was only in his third year that he began to find his academic feet; he placed thirteenth in a class of about ninety or so. However, as a student, he did publish in the *Harvard Magazine* and began to develop his philosophical bent and, most importantly, the distinctive writing style that was to hold him in such good stead later. As a student, he also honed his skills and charms as a ladies' man; he was considered something of a flirt.

When the Civil War broke out in 1861, Holmes enlisted for military service as quickly as he could. Under the influence of his mother, he had become an avowed abolitionist and thought it his moral duty to answer the call to arms in that cause's name. However, he declined an opportunity to serve with black Union soldiers; his abolitionist commitments were more intellectual than existential. Because he left for military training prior to graduation, Harvard threatened to deprive him of an honors degree and earned the considerable wrath of Holmes Sr. He was a member of Company A of the 20th Regiment, known also as the Harvard Regiment. The fact that he advanced through the ranks fairly quickly to the rank of lieutenant colonel was as much due to the depressingly rapid rate at which soldiers were being killed as to his leadership qualities.

Carte-de-visite (photograph) of Lieutenant Oliver Wendell Holmes Jr., in Civil War military uniform. Created by Silsbee, Case & Co, 11 November 1862. *Source:* Courtesy of Historical & Special Collections, Harvard Law School Library.

Involved in the Battle of Ball's Bluff, the Battle of Antietam, and other confrontations, Holmes led a charmed combat life compared with the rest of his brutalized compatriots. Although he was shot and wounded on three separate occasions, he survived relatively unscathed. After each wounding, he returned to Cambridge to convalesce for a couple of months. When his three years of service were complete in July 1864, he had had enough; he declined further promotion and did not reenlist. Witnessing the carnage at the Battle of the Wilderness, in which the dead were heaped five deep, was more than his already battle-hardened stomach could take.

Not surprisingly, these harrowing experiences left a deep scar on Holmes's psyche; he vacillated between reminiscing about war's grotesque brutality and about its glorious possibilities. It became something of a personal mission to justify his own survival and the death of so many others; he devoted himself to leading a life that was as worthwhile and beneficial as he could make it. As he was wont to state biblically, "whatsoever thy hand findeth to do, do it with thy might." With a keen mind, a driven ambition, and family connections to burn, Holmes set out to prove his mettle to himself, the world, and, as importantly, his father, Holmes Sr.

Holmes enrolled in Harvard Law School, from which he graduated in 1866 after the usual two years of study. That summer, he spent time in England and met many people of a similar station and outlook to the Holmeses, including John Stuart Mill, the philosopher and liberal. On his return, he passed the bar exams in early 1867 and soon rejoined the law firm of Chandler, Shattuck, and Thayer, where he had been a law clerk. In June 1872, he married his longtime companion, Fanny Dixwell, whom he had known since child-hood. It was a childless marriage (although they adopted and raised an orphaned cousin, Dorothy Upham) and one that gave Holmes much time to pursue his professional interests, but little else. Not always in the best of health, Fanny began to adopt a more reclusive style of life after a bout of rheumatic fever in 1896. Although she did more entertaining, as was expected of her, in Washington, she remained unenthusiastic. Nevertheless, she lived a further three decades. She died in April 1929.

Whatever the disappointment of his personal life, Holmes's professional career continued apace. He stayed with the Chandler firm until 1870, where he practiced mainly admiralty and commercial law for an established clientele. He left to commence practice in shared offices with his younger brother, Edward (who died in 1884 from compli-cations with asthma). However, as busy as Holmes was as a lawyer, he managed to find time to indulge his academic and intellectual leanings. Early on, he had learned that it is through "a laborious and somewhat painful period of pro-bation that the law opens a way to philosophy as well as anything else, if pursued far enough, and I hope to prove it before I die." He began teaching part-time at Harvard and began publishing in the late 1860s and early 1870s and never stopped. His first big break was becoming the editor of the *American Law Review* in 1870. He then edited a ver-sion of Kent's *Commentaries*, an annotated compendium of

federal and state law, in 1873. Although he was only supposed to be a junior editor, he wrested control of the project
from the more senior and renowned James Bradley Thayer,
a full-time Harvard professor. It was a calculated and typical move from a person who saw a main chance and had the
flair and determination to take it.

Continuing to practice, teach, and write (and jeopardiz-
ing his health by overwork), Holmes also remained active
in social and intellectual circles around Cambridge; he was
a frequent participant in the Metaphysical Club, along
with scientist and philosopher Charles Sanders Peirce; the
James brothers, psychologist William and novelist Henry;
and other local luminaries. All this came through in the
publication in 1881 of his magisterial *The Common Law*.
This was based on his twelve Lowell Lectures, named after
a Bostonian philanthropist. These were delivered on Tues-
day and Friday evenings in late 1880 at Huntington Hall.
The published collection is considered by many to be "the
best book on law ever written by an American." It is less a
summary of what the prevailing rules of common law were
and more a reflection on the method by which those rules
come about and are applied. As an effort to bring together
scientific insight and practical law, it is an intellectual tour
de force that provokes as much as it persuades. It remains
a canonical text of American jurisprudence broadly.

After the publication of *The Common Law* in 1881,
Holmes became a full-time professor at Harvard for the
first time in 1882. But he was only there for a few

months, because he was almost immediately appointed to the Massachusetts Supreme Judicial Court; an earlier effort to appoint him to the federal bench in 1878 had been unsuccessful. On taking office in January 1883, he was forty-one years old but still had almost fifty years of a judicial career ahead of him. He was a cautious judge and tended to follow precedent; he also continued to publish and lecture. He was made Chief Justice of the court in 1899. Three years later, in 1902, he was nominated for a position on the Supreme Court by the energetic and progressive President Theodore "Teddy" Roosevelt; he succeeded Justice Horace Gray. There was some good fortune in this, as President McKinley had lined up someone else but was assassinated, and this allowed the incoming Roosevelt to make a new choice. Holmes sat on the Supreme Court until his retirement in January 1932. By then, he was not only the oldest justice to serve in the Supreme Court's history, but also the one member who cannot be ignored in any assessment of credentials for entry into the pantheon of American legal greats.

When Oliver Wendell Holmes Jr. joined the Supreme Court, he had already developed a full-blown account of what he considered to be the common law's method and, by necessary implication, the role of its judicial expositors. For many, this would prove to be a distinct disadvantage; they would run the considerable risk of being hoisted, as judges, by their own intellectual petard. But Holmes seemed to relish the prospect. As a man of facts and action, he could now put reflective theory into bold action. If the proof of the pudding is in the eating, Holmes had his mouth full. Discovering how to digest and thrive on such rich fare was his main challenge as a judge.

While in law school, Holmes was already groping toward the basic pragmatist principles that would undergird his later and more sophisticated theoretical approach. He was convinced that there was no absolute or enduring notion of "truth" and that there was no fixed or objectively legitimate morality. Although this eventually earned him the label of a nihilist in some quarters, he held to a fairly demanding, if stern, personal morality; he simply did not believe that it had any claim to universal truth. He was prepared to extend similar privileges to others to develop their own morality in line with their material interests and emotional tastes. Although he was much more a relativist than a nihilist and lived his own life in an honorable way, this stance meant that he sailed very close to the idea that might was right and that law was one more tool to advance powerful interests in life's constant social struggle: "I believe that force, mitigated so far as it might be by good manners, is the *ultimate ratio*, and between two groups that want to make inconsistent kinds of worlds, I see no remedy except force." Indeed, perhaps forged in the savagery of the Civil War, this Hobbesian or even Nietzschean attitude reared its head in his judgments and incited much critical comment.

Although many young men shied away from doing so, Holmes challenged the prevailing orthodoxy from the get-go in making his mark in the legal profession. Contrary to the received wisdom at Harvard Law School in the 1860s and 1870s, he considered the common law to be "a ragbag of details" with no coherent structure. He challenged the view that law was a formal, self-contained, and scientific set of norms and principles and that lawyers should strive to detect its intellectual thread. But he did so in the name of a better science. Strongly influenced by the unsettling implications of an unmitigated Darwinian approach (as filtered through his classes and dealings with the biologist Asa Grey, the pragmatist Chauncey Wright, and other members of the ironically named Metaphysical Club), Holmes championed a more antiformalist approach to law that grounded itself on empirical knowledge and method; he railed against the legal process as an a priori method for arriving at legal truths, much like mathematics. Instead, he emphasized the more positivist idea that law was nothing more or less than the empirical product of human will in political matters.

The quintessence of this approach was captured in the oft-celebrated opening paragraph of *The Common Law* – "The life of the law has not been logic; it has been experience." For Holmes, justice was about the reasonableness of a decision in policy terms, not its logical consistency with existing rules; law was about the hard facts of social life as much as about normative fantasies of law as "a brooding omnipresence in the sky." Law was little more than "prophecies of what the courts will do in fact." Separating law from morality and eschewing metaphysical or moralizing niceties, he saw law as a vehicle for institutionalizing "what is expedient for the community" and as being representative of whatever a society's sovereign could successfully enforce. A corollary of this jurisprudential stance was that he saw law as best viewed from the predictive perspective of the "bad man" who "cares only for the material consequences which such knowledge enables him to predict, not as a good one, who finds his reasons in the vaguer sanctions of conscience."

Holmes played out these ideas across the range of legal doctrines. For him, the common law was an established body of accumulated community preferences that was always evolving and changing: "It is revolting to have no better reason for a rule of law than that so it was laid down in the time of Henry IV ... [and] still more revolting if the grounds upon which it was laid down have vanished long since, and the rule simply persists from blind imitation of the past." He was much more interested in shifting the focus of legal attention from teleological issues of moral duty to empirical matters of social consequences. For example, in understanding the law of contractual breach, he urged that there should be greater weight given to the actual consequences of breaking particular promises than the abstract quality of their moral making or validity. This led to what is now considered to be modern utilitarian orthodoxy that a contractor owes no duty to perform a contract but only to pay damages on its breach. The continuing potency of *The Common Law* is attributable to this utilitarian approach to law that found its most sympathetic and influential legacy in the modern law-and-economics movement.

Within this general understanding of law, the role of the judge was that of a facilitator and guardian who was to impose standards that would bring about the most desirable social consequences. From this instrumentalist and relativist stance, Holmes did not view the judge as a check on power; it was for legislatures to do what they thought best, and it was for judges to defer to that except in the most rare and extraordinary situations. This stance was not at all borne of any great respect for democracy – far from it. Holmes insisted that legislatures were much better placed to identify the practical reach of sovereign authority and to be the main author of "the story of a nation's development." For him, good judges are judges who are dispassionate and pragmatic; they model themselves not on a logician or moralist but on a social planner who connects social means with social ends in the most efficacious and effective ways. Exactly how all this would play out when moving from academic essays to judicial judgments was to be the test of Holmes's greatness and sincerity.

Although he considered that law was a prediction of what a judge would do, Holmes was not very predictable as a judge. He did little on the Massachusetts court that would persuade any uncommitted third party that he was destined for judicial greatness. In his almost twenty years on the court, although he made some important judgments, he kept his head down quite low and complied with his colleagues' overriding desire for unanimity; this is hardly unexpected for a person who had made much of judicial deference in his earlier work and writings. However, on his appointment to the Supreme Court in 1902, Holmes began to impress himself to a greater extent on the law and to give voice to his judicial and general philosophy. Indeed, the immediate circumstances of his appointment and early decisions tell a revealing tale.

Holmes was nominated on the recommendation of Senator Henry Cabot Lodge, a Massachusetts senator and statesman who had the ear of President Roosevelt. In addition to recognizing Holmes's undoubted legal talents, the battle-tried Roosevelt was impressed by Holmes's "Soldier's Faith" speech (a reminiscence of the Civil War in which Holmes waxed oratorically about "the incommunicable experience of war; we have felt, we still feel, the passion of life to its top"). Although the Senate unanimously confirmed the appointment, Holmes was disappointed by the fact that he was still very much seen as the son of his famous father (who had died in 1894) and considered "more brilliant than sound." Nevertheless, the president was confident that he could rely on Holmes to help shepherd through much of his political legislation against constitutional challenge. If Roosevelt had

Photograph portrait of Fanny Bowditch Dixwell Holmes, wife of Oliver Wendell Holmes Jr., c. 1870. *Source:* Courtesy of Historical & Special Collections, Harvard Law School Library.

scrutinized Holmes's writings more deeply and accurately, he would not have been so sanguine.

Holmes soon upset Roosevelt's expectations in the *Northern Securities* case in 1904. In his first dissent, he held that an alleged railroad cartel of the Great Northern and Northern Pacific Railway companies should be protected from government interference as an illegal monopoly. His rather dense and technical judgment took the elitist and probusiness line that there was no restraint of trade because "every concern monopolizes whatever business it does" and, as there was no intention to monopolize, there was nothing done "to exclude strangers to the combination from competing with it in some part of the business which it carries on." Although Holmes's dissent earned the lasting ire of Roosevelt and others, it fitted quite nicely with and followed from his Social Darwinian view that struggle, personal or economic, was the unavoidable and essential basis of social life: persons and their corporations should be left to pursue their own interests unhindered by legislative regulation. In hewing to his earlier views, Holmes was confirming, not confounding, his philosophical commitments.

But it was his commitment to judicial deference that began to take center stage in his adjudicative work. Beginning a practice of writing important (and later influential) dissents, Holmes stood firm against his colleagues in the now-infamous case of *Lochner* in 1905. A New York statute had set a maximum number of hours that could be worked in bakeries: ten daily and sixty weekly. This was a direct challenge to the exploitative and laissez-faire spirit that pervaded business. The constitutional issue was how to balance the police power of the state and the Fourteenth Amendment's guarantee of liberty – could the government limit people's right to purchase or sell labor? Striking down the legislation, the majority portrayed the law as "unreasonable, unnecessary and arbitrary interference with the right and liberty of the individual to contract"; there was little sensitivity to the need to protect workers' health and safety. Holmes dissented with a blistering three-paragraph judgment. In his inimitable style and with genuine passion, he laid out the judicial implications of his general jurisprudential stance:

> This case is decided upon an economic theory which a large part of the country does not entertain. If it were a question whether I agreed with that theory I should desire to study it further and long before making up my mind. But I do not conceive that to be my duty, because I strongly believe that my agreement or disagreement has nothing to do with the right of a majority to embody their opinions in law. It is settled by various decisions of this Court that State constitutions and state laws may regulate life in many ways which we as legislators might think as injudicious or if you like as tyrannical as this, and which equally with this interfere with the liberty to contract. . . . The Fourteenth Amendment does not enact Mr. Herbert Spencer's Social Statics. . . .
>
> Some of these laws embody convictions or prejudices which judges are likely to share. Some may not. But a constitution is not intended to embody a particular economic theory, whether of paternalism and the organic relation of the citizen to the State or of laissez faire. It is made for people of fundamentally differing views, and the accident of our finding certain opinions natural and familiar or novel and even shocking ought not to conclude our judgment upon the

question whether statutes embodying them conflict with the Constitution of the United States.

I think that the word liberty in the Fourteenth Amendment is perverted when it is held to prevent the natural outcome of a dominant opinion, unless it can be said that a rational and fair man necessarily would admit that the statute proposed would infringe fundamental principles as they have been understood by the traditions of our people and our law. It does not need research to show that no such sweeping condemnation can be passed upon the statute before us.

Most of Holmes's distinctive motifs are present here – community opinion, sovereign will, relativist values, ideological indifference, and the like. It says much about his approach to judging that he had no real liking for the kind of paternalistic welfare that the New York laws represented; he thought that they were ill fated and ill advised as efforts at social engineering. Although he dissented in *Lochner* and other similar cases, he also joined with the majority and occasionally wrote judgments that struck down some economic regulation. His approach was less about an allegiance to any substantive political doctrines and more about his commitment to a particular conception of judicial decision making and social theory. It was only after his retirement and in the throes of the New Deal era that Holmes's dissent came to be regarded as the gold standard for how judges should handle their judicial responsibilities in matters of economic regulation. The ghost of Holmes's *Lochner* dissent still stalks the halls of academe and the chambers of judicial offices.

Another lasting legacy of Holmes is in the area of free speech. In a series of decisions that dominated the second half of his tenure on the Supreme Court, he made an uncompromising defense of the Constitution's First Amendment. Ironically, he is most celebrated for his articulation of the "clear and present danger" limits to free speech. In *Schenck* in 1919, he stated that "the question in every case is whether the words used are used in such circumstances and are of such a nature as to create a clear and present danger that they will bring about the substantive evils that Congress has a right to prevent." He followed this up in *Abrams*, another political pamphleteering case, with a dissent that introduced the need to preserve "the free trade of ideas": "[people] may come to believe even more than they believe the very foundations of their own conduct that the ultimate good desired is better reached by free trade in ideas – that the best test of truth is the power of the thought to get itself accepted in the competition of the market." Again, Holmes had little sympathy for the views of the pamphleteers in this and other cases – comparing them with "the right of a donkey to drool" – and would likely have opted for persecution of such views if given his own personal druthers. But he was prepared to accept and act on the conviction that all views, no matter how nonsensical or wrongheaded, "should be given their chance and have their way."

In line with his early antiformalist views, Holmes also remained true to his understanding of the common law as a social organism, not an otherworldly tablet. In *Black and White Taxi Co. v. Brown & Yellow Taxi Co.* in 1928, one taxi company was sued to prevent the alleged interference with a contract of exclusivity between another taxi company and the owner of the property. The defendant taxi company replied that the contract was prohibited by state law and that the plaintiff taxi company incorporated out of state "for the fraudulent purpose of evading [state] laws." The majority held that, as no local laws were involved, the validity of the contract depended on the applicable rules of a general or federal common law; these took precedence over local laws and their content was to be ascertained by the Supreme Court and other federal courts.

Holmes had no truck with this approach. True to his academic views, he resisted the claim that there was a general federal common law that took priority over the legislated and common law of individual states when those cases were appealed to federal courts. Vindicated by the later *Erie* case in 1938, at least in substance if not in rhetoric, Holmes offered the opinion that

> [i]t is very hard to resist the impression that there is one august corpus [of common law]. . . . If there were such a transcendental body of law outside of any particular state but obligatory within it unless and until changed by statute, the courts of the United States might be right in using their

independent judgment as to what it was. But there is no such body of law. The fallacy and illusion that I think exist consist in supposing that there is this outside thing to be found.

Holmes's continuing adherence to his utilitarian and Darwinian views did not always take him in the best of directions. Perhaps his most infamous (and many would say reprehensible) decision was in *Buck v. Bell* in 1927. The eighteen-year-old Carrie Buck was fighting a sterilization order under a Virginia statute. Writing for a majority of the court, Holmes upheld the law that promoted the idea that a patient's health and the society's welfare might best be protected "by the sterilization of mental defectives, under careful safeguard." Describing the applicant as "the daughter of a feeble minded mother . . . and the mother of a feeble minded child," he relied on a strict utilitarian notion of civic sacrifice:

> We have seen more than once that the public welfare may call upon the best citizens for their lives. It would be strange if it could not call upon those who already sap the strength of the State for these lesser sacrifices, often not felt to be such by those concerned, in order to prevent our being swamped with incompetence. It is better for all the world, if instead of waiting to execute degenerate offspring for crime, or to let them starve for their imbecility, society can prevent those who are manifestly unfit from continuing their kind. . . . Three generations of imbeciles are enough.

For Holmes, this endorsement of eugenics, at least of a negative kind, was entirely warranted. Popular among the scientific and cultural elites in which Holmes moved, this line of thinking was also recommended as a matter of the state's sovereign expression of popular views and the need to take a clear-eyed view of society's struggle. The problem was that, even if the Constitution did not "enact Mr. Herbert Spencer's Social Statics," the judgment did seem to favor a similarly harsh and calculating vision of genetic purity; it is Holmes's most reviled decision. It was picked up by some lawyers at the postwar Nuremberg trials to defend some German Nazis. Also, as a result of this decision, sterilization rates in the United States climbed. It was not until the 1960s that sterilizations fell almost completely out of favor, even though their enabling laws persisted. Virginia's sterilization law remained on the books until 1974.

Time has shown that Holmes's lasting influence is less about the impact of specific judgments (which was considerable) and more about the effect of his overall approach and style. As with many leading judges, the whole was greater than the sum of its parts. Consolidated over his lengthy tenure on the Supreme Court, his judgments blended a writing technique with an overarching pragmatic method (i.e., what works?) that stands out among his contemporaries; it opened up an important space for those who followed and who wished to resist the pressures to conform. But his enduring appeal can be found in the fact that, although he generated as much criticism as praise, his judicial efforts cannot be ignored; they must be engaged with and taken seriously. When viewed in its fullness and its appropriate historical context, his contribution stands out as capturing and, at the same time, redefining the nature and performance of the judicial role.

As one would anticipate, the response to Holmes has been both strong and divided. His work and his values have elicited spirited debate on many levels and along many axes; there are few legal or historical observers who have been indifferent to him. In many ways, this sharp division is not so much evidence against Holmes as further proof of Holmes's greatness.

Holmes was difficult to categorize along some simplistic conservative–liberal spectrum. Whatever his personal views on a variety of topics (and he had many), he took it as his judicial duty to defer to much that the government promoted as desirable public policy; he upheld legislation whether it was progressive or regressive. As much as he sided with pamphleteers and unionists on occasion, he also turned a cold shoulder to social activists and the dispossessed. For example, in the 1911 decision *Bailey v. Alabama*, he decided it was fair to make a black man do hard labor for breaching a labor contract when he could not pay restitution; the fact that it was more or less "a kind of limited slavery," as Holmes previously put it, did not matter. This not only contradicted his view on contractual remedies in *The Common Law* but was also crudely insensitive to America's racist past. Moreover, as an avowed atheist and relativist, he did not curry much favor with traditional conservatives. In terms of his political agenda, Holmes was, as in so much, his own man; he cut across customary allegiances and defied easy pigeonholing.

A continuing charge against Holmes is that he not only tolerated the harsh realities of the world but also welcomed them too openly into the judicial corridors of power. It is one thing to view life through a Darwinian lens and see struggle and conflict as the inevitable dynamic of the world. But it is another thing entirely to revel in the resulting savagery and turn it into a guiding article of Nietzschean faith in which the weak succumb to the powerful for no other reason than that they are powerful. In some ways, Holmes seemed captive to the nihilistic image of the social being that he had sketched in his postwar years; he seemed unwilling or unable to break out of this confining glumness. Although he fulfilled his social obligations on the Washington scene, his personal isolation there merely reinforced this pessimistic understanding of people's opportunities and outlook. As one commentator has noted, although it is difficult to sympathize too much with such a successful and ambitious person, "perhaps a lonely and childless man with few, if any, real friends deserves more pity than condemnation."

Sadly, Holmes became the callous embodiment of the alienated figure of the bad man that he had identified and that populated his judicial and juristic musings. His sense

Justice Oliver Wendell Holmes, c. 1930. *Source:* Library of Congress – Prints and Photographs Division [LC-USZ62-47817].

of what it was to be a good person and a good lawyer seemed to amount to little more than being ardent about one's own interests and attentive to the consequences of one's actions. This seems an attenuated and unappetizing account of social morality. Indeed, from a jurisprudential point of view, whatever the ethical shortcomings of this relativistic approach, it

seemed to give the lie to Holmes's positivistic claim that law
and morality were somehow separate and distinct. Large
parts of Holmes's judicial opinions are given over to advancing or at least facilitating the tooth-and-claw amorality in
which power was the only currency in the social circulation
that he recognized at work in American culture.

This approach seems most clearly on display in Holmes's
ruthless judgment in *Buck v. Bell* – "Three generations of
imbeciles are enough." However, it must be remembered
that Holmes's judgment in that case was written on behalf
of all his colleagues except one. In adopting such a stance,
he was not an outlier or misfit. Although more rigorous and
unforgiving than many, he embodied a social philosophy that
received strong support among the established classes. For
good and bad, Holmes was more a man of his times than
many are prepared to admit or allow. Even though he has
become known as "the great dissenter," he dissented much
less often than many think. During his first eight years on
the Massachusetts court, he registered only two dissents.
Moreover, only 72 out of his approximately 1,000 opinions
during his career on the Supreme Court were in dissent. It
was more the timing and positioning of his dissents than
their quantity that gave Holmes this reputation.

Of course, all this raises the perennial problem of how
to evaluate the values and views of those who lived in times
different and distant to our own – are we to ignore context
and prevailing mores? Are we to give people the benefit of
the historical doubt? It seems that the standard perhaps

should be higher for those who hold offices of authority and who consider themselves to be the makers, not the followers, of social fashion. Holmes falls somewhere in between. Although he can hardly claim that he was powerless by position or personality not to go with the moral flow (as his whole juristic oeuvre was very much against the traditional grain), he cannot be expected to stand entirely outside his social context. On this basis, Holmes must take a large share of the responsibility and blame for his views and values. And this he did.

The crucial issue at stake is whether this is sufficient to tarnish Holmes's reputation to the extent that it disallows him from being treated as a truly great judge. For my part, I come to the conclusion that he remains a great judge in spite of his values and social philosophy. The parade of horribles that is usually marched out to damn him is indeed most troubling. But there is still so much to support his case to be included in the ranks of great judges. The self-assured way he went about his responsibilities, the judicial courage of his jurisprudential convictions, his unconventional mode of legal analysis, and the continuing modern impact of his constitutional stance combine to set him apart from most other Supreme Court judges. And his style of judgment writing cannot be ignored. Holmes had a definite and distinctive way with words. Despite his early pronouncement that "the law is not the place for the artist or the poet," he brought to his judicial duties a rhetorical artistry that often ran to the poetic as much as the analytical. Recognizing that persuasion was the ultimate test of the good judge, he was prepared to utilize every tool at his disposal to make his case. In style and substance, Oliver Wendell Holmes was his own man, with all that entailed.

In January 1932, at ninety years of age, Holmes's judicial colleagues persuaded him that it was time to go. After submitting a resignation letter to Chief Justice Hughes, he left the Supreme Court with a simple and teary "I won't be in tomorrow." This departure was understated and somewhat uncharacteristic for a man who had become a national institution in his own lifetime. Holmes was, as is hinted in the chapter, a major public figure for his time in a way that few justices over history have been. Even on his ninetieth birthday, he was renowned enough to be accorded a radio broadcast in which he said that "the race is over, but the work never is done while the power to work remains." He was, in short, industrious and influential to the very end.

Of course, it helped that Holmes's life traversed a period in which America had moved from a youngish war-ravaged nation to a world power. And it is to his credit that he played a formative role in that history as soldier, jurist, judge, and all-around citizen. Although born under privileged circumstances, he did not waste his talents or his opportunities. When he died from pneumonia (like his wife and many others) on 6 March 1935, two days short of his ninety-first birthday, Wendy did so confident in the knowledge that he had achieved the one thing that had never been far from his mind, conscious and unconscious – he had become more famous than his father.

In the past seventy-five years, Holmes has become a larger-than-life and extravagant figure of American history. A 1944 fictionalized biography, *Yankee from Olympus*, by Catherine Bowen, was a longtime bestseller and added luster to the Holmesian mystique. There also was a play written about him by Emmet Lavery in 1946, titled *The Magnificent Yankee*. In 1950, Holmes even made it to Hollywood. Lavery's play was turned into a movie by director John Sturges; Louis Calhern received an Oscar nomination for his portrayal of Holmes. Holmes was included in the U.S. Postal Service's Prominent Americans Series (1965–1978) and featured as the face of a fifteen-cent stamp. Since the extensive collection of Holmes's papers and correspondence was made public in 1985 by Harvard Law School, there have been several more and competing biographies on Holmes that strive to capture the singular character that was Oliver Wendell Holmes Jr. The fact that he still defies simple analysis merely adds fuel to the mythological fire.

Oliver Wendell Holmes is buried in Arlington National Cemetery. As he had no close family, he bequeathed most of his large residuary estate to the U.S. government. He had taken great pains to preserve his bloody and tattered Civil War uniform and the three bullets that were extracted from his injuries. The effects of that conflict and the personal toll that it took on Holmes cannot be underestimated. In his own

James Atkin was one of those strong characters who was a product of his own social milieu as well as a major influence on it. Although he stood out from the crowd, he never sought to put himself above or beyond ordinary people. In his long and illustrious career, he managed to hold on to and celebrate the original basis of the common law – that it arose from the customs of the common people and was intended to serve their best interests. As such, he took seriously the special judicial undertaking to develop the law in line with the ideals of the society of which he was such a part. He was an ordinary man in the best and most extraordinary sense of the description.

Although James Richard Atkin was born in Queensland, Australia, he was very much a Welshman through and through. His life began in straitened circumstances in the mid-Victorian years in the Southern Hemisphere and, running through two world wars in Europe, culminated in his beloved North Wales after a stellar legal career. That he achieved as much as he did owed much to the huge and acknowledged influence of several women in his life – his grandmother, mother, wife, and six daughters. In his seventy-seven years, he went from a precarious fatherless existence to become one of the most revered judges in the English legal tradition.

"Dick" was the first son of the Irishman Robert Travers Atkin and his Welsh wife, Mary Elizabeth ("Tilly") Ruck.

The young couple married in 1864 and emigrated to Australia in 1865 to seek, along with so many others, a new beginning. Robert was from old money, but the family fortunes had taken a distinct downturn. Tilly was from a more modest background in North Wales. The plan was to buy and operate a sheep farm. They established themselves at Herbert's Creek, near Rockhampton in Queensland, almost four hundred miles north of Brisbane. After an initial hint at agricultural success, their sheep-raising venture floundered; this was partly attributable to Robert suffering a disabling fall from his horse. For the next couple of years, Robert and Tilly moved between Rockhampton and Brisbane.

Robert became editor of a local newspaper and began to dabble in Queensland politics. Although unsuccessful in the sheep-farming business, he nevertheless achieved some status and was befriended by William Hemmant, a prosperous Queensland merchant and established politician. Under his sponsorship, Robert became a member of the Legislative Assembly for East Moreton. At the same time that Robert was beginning to make a real name for himself, Tilly was rearing their family. James Richard was born on Tank Street in North Quay, Brisbane, on 28 November 1867. He was the oldest of three brothers; Walter Steward was born in May 1869 and Robert Laurence in September 1870.

In short order, Robert soon became the leader of the Liberal Party. However, as Robert's political star was set to rise even higher, tragedy struck. At the end of May 1872, Robert died of consumption at the age of thirty. In his last few months, he had been taken care of by the generosity of Hemmant, who spent a tidy sum on Robert's medical attention in his dying months. Shortly after his death, a public memorial was erected by the Hibernian Society of Queensland in Robert's honor; it read, "His days were few but his labours and attainments bore the same stamp of a wise maturity." However, the Atkin family's dealings with the Hemmants were by no means finished.

A year or so before Robert's death, Tilly and her young sons had left Queensland and sailed back to the United Kingdom. The precise reasons for this dramatic turn of events are unclear. But a combination of homesickness, an ailing child (Robert), a struggling marriage, and a dying husband likely persuaded Tilly that the future of her sons was more assured back home in Wales than in distant Australia. It was a brave and risky move. The four-year-old Dick had little later recollection of this traumatic period other than the length of the voyage home, the caged animals on board their ship, and his welcome back home by his affectionate Welsh grandparents.

By the time Robert died, his family had taken up residence at Tilly's parents' house, Pantlludw, on the River Dovey in Meirionnydd, North Wales; it was a modest slate-roofed cottage in a rural and mostly Welsh-speaking region of the country. Here, Dick and his brothers fell under the considerable influence of their formidable *nain*, Mary Anne Ruck. She was apparently descended from Owain Glyndwr, who was a fourteenth-century lordly scourge of the English

Undated photograph portrait of Lord Atkin. *Source:* Courtesy of Historical & Special Collections, Harvard Law School Library.

and an authentic Welsh folk hero. When combined with her reputed gypsy blood on her mother's side, this made her a special and combustible character. A demanding, no-nonsense, but affectionate woman, she expected much of her grandchildren and shared her learning, zest for life, and sense of fairness freely; she was very literate and emancipated for a woman of her generation. Although her effect on the growing and inquisitive Dick cannot be underestimated, he also benefited from the care and connections of his mother's new husband and his stepfather, Lieutenant Colonel Thomas Ruddiman Steuart. Thirty years older than Tilly, he became the father figure that Dick so desired.

Something of a precocious young lad, Dick went away to Friars School in Bangor, about seventy miles away, when he was eight. The headmaster, Mr. Lloyd, recognized great academic potential in Atkin and arranged for his pupil to accompany him to the more prestigious Christ College in Brecon, mid-Wales, a few years later. A little nearer to home, Dick thrived and exceeded any reasonable expectations that Mr. Lloyd or his family could have had for him. Enjoying his classes and his sporting pursuits (with tennis being his forte), he retained a fond connection to the college throughout his life and returned often. Following a happy and successful time at the college, the sixteen-year-old Atkin won a demyship to Magdalen College, Oxford, in 1884. This was a scholarship for less affluent students and put him among the ranks of other holders, like Oscar Wilde, T. E. Lawrence, and the future Lord Denning. Unfortunately, his time at Magdalen was not the most satisfying; he felt that he was too young and too gauche to do well in this upper-class enclave. Perhaps because of this social unease, he performed less confidently than he might otherwise have done and narrowly missed a first-class degree in classics and humanities. Nevertheless, in his later life, he was delighted when the college's law society was named after him in 1936.

From Oxford, Atkin had to decide on some sort of career for himself. Choosing law more by default than anything else, he joined Gray's Inn, one of the four institutions at which aspiring lawyers had to be a member to become a barrister. His choice of Gray's was determined by the fact that the only lawyer he knew was his grandfather's cousin, Edwyn Jones, who had a thriving legal practice there. But Atkin's affiliation with Gray's was to be a long and mutually supportive one. At different times, he became the treasurer of the inn (its nominal and annually elected head) and was for many years master of the library as well as master of the moots (mock appeal presentations by students); he edited and published *The Moot Book of Gray's Inn*, of which he was particularly proud. This legacy is honored still today by the Atkin Scholarship, from which an award of £5,000 is made annually to the most promising young advocate.

At this stage, Atkin had no legal training at all, like many of his fellow students. The expectation was that talented young men (there were no women members at this time) would become proficient in law by their informal training as pupils to more senior barristers. Under the tutelage of Edwyn Jones, he completed his bar exams and was called to the bar in 1891. Living a bare-bones existence, he managed to obtain pupillage with Thomas Scrutton, who was later to become one of his colleagues on the Court of Appeal; his fellow pupils were Frank MacKinnon and Robert Wright, who also both went on to illustrious judicial careers. From there, he secured chambers on the first floor of 3 Pump Court in the

Temple; barristers could join colleagues in shared chambers but could not form partnerships or firms.

Atkin married Lucy Elizabeth ("Lizzie") Hemmant in 1893, shortly after he had been called to the bar. Their romance was a quintessential small world occurrence: Dick had met Lizzie when her father, the same William Hemmant who had helped care for Dick's dying father in Queensland, had relocated to London; she had been born within twelve days of Atkin's birthday and one hundred yards of his birthplace. By all reports, she was very much in the mold of Atkin's own mother and grandmother – a strong, dynamic, and irrepressible woman of independent views who was also a gifted amateur pianist. They made an exceptional couple and had six daughters and two sons. They divided their time between their London home in posh Kensington and a substantial property, Craig-y-don, in the less heralded Aberdyfi in Merionydd, where Atkin could be an ordinary local. Although their eldest son died in the First World War, their other children went on to lead successful lives; one daughter, Nancy, became an actress, and the youngest, Rosaline, became a Gray's Inn lawyer, to Atkin's great pride. Elizabeth and Richard (although not as tempestuous or infamous as their celebrity counterparts, Taylor and Burton) had a solid and supportive marriage until Lizzie's death in 1939.

In his first few years at the bar, it was a hardscrabble existence for Atkin; he had no real connections to the larger legal or business world. In his first five years, he made less than £100 annually. Fortunately, he was able to call on Lizzie and her father's generous support to buy time for his career to take off. And luckily it did. With help and contacts from his father-in-law's export business and commercial network, he began to build a career and reputation for himself. Through one of Hemmant's acquaintances, Mr. Grant, who was the Official Assignee of the London Stock Exchange, Atkin secured not only a more steady flow of commercial cases but also those that enabled him to show his professional mettle; he was quietly assured rather than flashily brash in his style. Atkin took advantage of the fact that he had his foot firmly in the establishment door. He cultivated a flourishing practice. By the turn of the century, he was one of the busiest barristers in London and founded his own set of chambers located at 1 Hare Court. Shortly before he became a king's counsel in 1906 at the age of thirty-nine, he caught the lawyerly eye of the future prime minister, H. H. Asquith, who sat as a commercial arbitrator. Such a liaison would pay a handsome dividend as Atkin's name began to be mentioned as a possible candidate for judicial office.

Atkin was appointed as a judge of the King's Bench Division by Lord Haldane, Asquith's Lord Chancellor, in 1913 at the age of forty-five. Not only was this celebrated by his fellow lawyers, but it led to a public demonstration of affectionate support on the Aberdyfi waterfront. Although Atkin missed the hustle and bustle of his lawyering life, his appointment was to begin a thirty-one-year judicial career in which he would soon find his feet and become one of the judicial community's most exemplary members. He became known for his restrained but firm courtroom manner, and he demonstrated balanced judgment in his decisions. Although he broke no new legal ground, he acquitted himself with sufficient distinction that he was promoted to the Court of Appeal in 1919. He found this position to be unsatisfying, as he was neither fish nor fowl; he did not get to deal directly with litigants, nor did he have the final say on the big legal issues of the day. Nonetheless, he proved to be a sound and respected colleague who was prized for his efficient work ethic. He primarily sat with his old pupil master, Thomas Scrutton, and Lord Bankes. Although Atkin retained enormous esteem for Scrutton, they were usually at odds in their preferred disposition of cases. As Lord Denning phrased it in Atkin's entry in the *Dictionary of National Biography*, "they fought for the body of Bankes."

After nine years on the Court of Appeal, in 1928 Atkin was appointed to succeed Lord Atkinson in the House of Lords. He took the title of Baron Atkin of Aberdovey (the Anglicized version of Aberdyfi); it was a suitable tribute to and recognition of his humble and influential ties. Up to then, he had done little that was to mark him as anything other than a highly competent and very well-regarded member of the senior judiciary. However, there were some signs that he might finally begin to raise his game and set himself apart from his colleagues. Although he lost the fight for "the body of Bankes" in two particular cases and, therefore, had to write dissenting judgments, he showed a civil liberties sensibility that was rare at that time. In the 1920 case of *Meering v. Graham-White Aviation Co. Ltd.*, he wanted to hold that a person could sue for false imprisonment even if he was not fully aware of his confinement at the time. And, in the same year, in *Everett v. Griffiths*, he maintained that a man detained in an insane asylum on inadequate grounds had a civil claim for damages against the asylum's board of governors.

These two dissents represent small, promising sparks that Atkin would need to fuel and fan into larger fires if he were to light up a more compelling path to judicial greatness. And, in his sixteen years on the Judicial Committee of the House of Lords, Atkin would rise to the challenge and confound many observers. Although his claim to be counted among the coveted ranks of great judges owes a great deal to two particular judgments, it is his overall approach to the judicial task and his general performance that recommend him. Although less prominent and more restrained than some of his professional equals, Lord Atkin slowly but surely gave full expression to a principled style of adjudication that was firmly anchored on the guiding values of ordinary men and women. The fact that this approach is now a fairly common mode of decision making ought not to reduce the power and originality of its initial performance.

A large part of Lord Atkin's claim to judicial greatness derives from his judgment in *Donoghue v. Stevenson*. This is arguably the most well-known case in the whole of the common law canon; its influence reached to all corners of the common law world. In August 1928, May Donoghue became ill after she drank a bottle of ginger beer bought for her by a friend at a local Glasgow café. In a novel legal claim, her campaigning lawyer, Walter Leechman, sought to hold the drink's manufacturer liable, even though May had no contract with the manufacturer (or anyone else for that matter). Her initial victory at trial was overturned by the Scottish Court of Sessions. However, once granted a petition to appeal in forma pauperis, May's claim (which was never proved as a matter of fact) was set to make legal headlines.

By the time Donoghue's appeal came around in late 1931, Lord Atkin had earned a solid reputation for himself as a keen intellect with a desire for justice; he regularly sought to ensure that he put the attainment of justice above rote adherence to the law. Moving easily between the professional and academic worlds, he was a frequent lecturer at law faculties. Indeed, in a speech to King's College, London, on 28 October 1931, a mere six weeks before hearing the arguments in Donoghue's case, he talked about the close relation between law and morality. In retrospect, some maintain that his speech foretold the fate of Donoghue's claim and the future of negligence law. He concluded his speech by stating that "I doubt whether the whole of the law of tort could not be comprised in the golden maxim to do unto your neighbour as you would that he should do unto you." It is this openly biblical theme of neighborliness that splices together his judgment in the appeal (and much else in his career).

In a wide-ranging opinion delivered in May 1932, Lord Atkin took the view that the judge's task was to detect the underlying legal principles of which the case law was merely illustrative: "[I]n English law there must be, and is, some general conception of relations giving rise to a duty of care, of which the particular cases found in the books are but instances." In line with this general sentiment, he analyzed the relevant cases and spotted a thread that was slowly emerging and that animated the continuing development of recent law. In one of the most majestic as well as most influential statements of legal principle in the common law world, Lord Atkin said:

> The rule that you are to love your neighbour becomes in law, you must not injure your neighbour; and the lawyer's question, Who is my neighbour? receives a restricted reply. You must take reasonable care to avoid acts or omissions which you can reasonably foresee would be likely to injure your neighbour. Who, then, in law is my neighbour? The answer seems to be – persons who are so closely and directly affected by my act that I ought reasonably to have them in contemplation as being so affected when I am directing my mind to the acts or omissions which are called in question.

With this sweeping statement of principle, Lord Atkin set in motion an interpretive process that continues to this day

across the legal world. For some, Lord Atkin's way of proceeding was inappropriate and unprofessional; it was seen to
usher in a litigious culture. He was chastised by his judicial
colleagues in the case, Lords Buckmaster and Tomlin, for
extending civil liability well beyond its natural or desirable
limits – "If one step, why not fifty?" But, for others, it leavened the law's high-mindedness with a much-needed dose of
common sense. Lord Atkin was praised by the eminent Sir
Frederick Pollock in the *Law Quarterly Review* for "overriding the scruples of English colleagues who could not emancipate themselves from the pressure of a supposed current of
authority in the English Courts." Insofar as it pierced public consciousness, there was warm approval. Whereas the
newspaper the *Scotsman* wrote that the decision "should be
welcomed by the public," the *Law Times* said that the decision was "revolutionary" and represented a "radical change"
in tort law that was "strictly in accord with the needs of
modern economic times."

Yet the importance and significance of the case was not
automatic and had to be earned over time. This it has done
over the years; it remains the fountainhead of authority
for negligence liability in the United Kingdom, the Commonwealth, and, to a lesser extent, the United States. The
charm of Lord Atkin's opinion was its suggestive and broad
language; it pointed in certain directions but left open its
precise meaning in particular circumstances. Like great
works of literature, Lord Atkin's *Donoghue* opinion left much

Portrait of Lord Atkin by Sir Oswald Birley, c. 1933. *Source:* By kind permission of the Masters of the Bench of the Honourable Society of Gray's Inn.

to be determined by its later readers; it came to be a great case not only because of its profundity but also because of its profligacy. In short, it is because of, not in spite of, his opinion's rather Delphic or oracular quality that it launched the neighbor principle and its author on the path to legal greatness. And it was its invocation of ordinary and common values that assured it a robust place in the law.

However, Atkin's portfolio of legal decisions is much more extensive than the focus on *Donoghue* suggests. He made several fundamental contributions to the private law of obligations; his interventions were marked by a strong grasp of the practicalities of commerce and a sensitivity to theoretical nuance. In the 1932 case of *Bell v. Lever Brothers* on mistake in contract, he staked out a jurisprudential stance that gave priority to the parties' actual bargain – "Nothing is more dangerous than to allow oneself liberty to construct for the parties contracts which they have not in terms made by importing implications which would appear to make the contract more business-like or more just." Again, in *Arcos v. Ronaasen & Son* in 1933, he insisted that the parties were entitled to demand strict, not merely substantial, compliance with the contractual terms; this position was approved and introduced into legislation by Parliament. He was also active in framing the scope of defamation actions and, in *Sim v. Stretch* in 1936, he coined the definitive phrase for determining defamatory statements – "[W]ould the words tend to lower the plaintiff in the estimation of right-thinking members of society generally."

Atkin's contributions were not restricted to private law. His other outstanding judgment was in the 1942 public law case of *Liversidge v. Anderson*, which dealt with the controversial issue of the accountability of the executive to the judiciary as well as parliament. His defiant wartime opinion still has a powerful resonance that has become especially timely again today. In May 1940 in the middle of intense hostilities with Germany, a man known as Robert Liversidge (whose real name was Jack Perlzweig) was imprisoned without trial by the home secretary, Sir John Anderson; he had been given authority under the Emergency Powers (Defence) Act of 1939 to detain people whom he had "reasonable cause to believe" were "of hostile origin . . . or to have been recently concerned in acts prejudicial to the public safety or the defence of the realm." The secretary refused to disclose the grounds for that belief. A majority of the House of Lords took the view that, as long as there was no evidence that the secretary had acted in bad faith, the decision did not lend itself to judicial review, because the judges had no business questioning executive decisions in matters of national security: "[I]t is right so to interpret emergency legislation as to promote rather than to defeat its efficacy."

Atkin stood fast and refused to join his four colleagues in their decision. He wrote a strong and passionate dissenting opinion that insisted that the home secretary was required to have and disclose reasonable grounds for Liversidge's detention. Disparaging the majority's Humpty Dumpty view of language ("[W]hen I use a word, it means just what I choose it to mean, neither more nor less"), he maintained that the legislation could not be construed to give the secretary uncontrolled discretion. After chastising his fellow judges for being "when face to face with claims involving the liberty of the subject . . . more executive-minded than the executive," he laid out the justification for his own position in unequivocal and principled terms:

> In this country amidst the clash of arms the laws are not silent. They may be changed, but they speak the same language in war as in peace. It has always been one of the pillars of freedom, one of the principles of liberty for which on recent authority we are now fighting, that the judges are no respecters of persons and stand between the subject and any attempted encroachments on his liberty by the executive, alert to see that any coercive action is justified in law. In this case I have listened to arguments which might have been addressed acceptably to the Court of Kings Bench in the time of Charles I.

> I protest, even if I do it alone, against a strained construction put upon words with the effect of giving an uncontrolled power of imprisonment to the Minister.

As a sole dissenter and in the middle of the war, taking such a stance demanded courage as well as conviction; Liversidge was not a sympathetic character. Atkin's was a far from popular position then (and now). He had to resist the insistent overtures from the Lord Chancellor, Viscount Simon, to join the majority or, at least, tone down his dissenting opinion. Indeed, it is often reported that his fellow law lords (Maugham, Macmillan, Wright, and Romer) declined to have lunch with him ever again; Maugham even wrote to the *Times* to air his misgivings publically. Also, Atkin's brave declaration in *Liversidge* stands in stark contrast to the wartime decisions in the United States, where its judges were, in cases like *Quirin* and *Korematsu*, long on deference to the military and short on upholding individual rights. Atkin could take the critical heat as well as warm compliments.

Atkin's bold deportment on *Liversidge* says much for his jurisprudence and marks him as a judge who was prepared to place principle ahead of popularity; he put his personal money where his judicial mouth was. Nevertheless, he refused to be swayed from his deep-seated commitments, which he had developed and exhibited in earlier but less pressing decisions. As a later law lord, Johan Steyn, noted when speaking of Atkin's opinion, "while courts must take into account the relative constitutional competence of branches of government to decide particular issues, they must never, on constitutional grounds, surrender the constitutional duties placed on them." Atkin's initial stance still stands as a beacon in the contemporary struggle to balance national security and civil liberties.

Occurring near the end of Atkin's judicial career, the *Liversidge* dissent stands as a fitting landmark to his immense and deserved stature as a judge. And time has tended to vindicate Atkin's views. Notwithstanding Lord Denning's preference for a judicial hands-off policy in regard to ministerial discretion in national security matters, the British courts have retreated from the *Liversidge* decision, but they have been reluctant to overrule it entirely. The closest the

House of Lords came was in *I.R.C. v. Rossminster Ltd.*, in which Lord Diplock stated that "the time has come to acknowledge openly that the majority of this House [in *Liversidge*] . . . were expediently and, at that time, perhaps, excusably, wrong and the dissenting speech of Lord Atkin was right." Although some countries, such as Singapore and Malaysia, have stayed with the majority's view, other Commonwealth jurisdictions have preferred Atkin's position. If greatness is about continuing to exert real influence after one has left the bench, then Atkin's judgments in *Liversidge* and *Donoghue* can make a genuine claim to be considered to be some of the most influential in the history of twentieth-century law; they are the main pivot around which contemporary debate still swings.

Atkin insisted that, for all the public responsibilities and profile of his judicial position, a judge should be entitled (and perhaps required) to lead an entirely private and anonymous life. Indeed, he liked nothing better than to be in Aberdyfi with his family and its local community. He did service as a local magistrate in Merionydd. And he was particularly fond of sitting in juvenile matters; he thought of justice and law being better served by a young petty thief receiving a parental spanking than by the same thief receiving an official detention. But he was happiest on the tennis court, on the golf links, at the cricket field, in a bridge pairing, or reading a good detective novel. In so many ways, he strove to be that reasonable man that the common law so loved and honored; this was in contrast to the sizeable gap between Holmes's reasonable man and his own life (see Chapter 4). He continued to ride the bus around London throughout his life, as he thought driving was much too dangerous an activity. But, for all his intellectual gifts and institutional standing, he liked a good chuckle at the antics of music hall characters like George Robey and Gordon Harker; he was reputed to have attended the cockney-inspired musical *Me and My Girl* more than a dozen times and sang (and danced) heartily the show-stopping number "The Lambeth Walk."

However, notwithstanding his cherished desire to keep his public and private life separate, it is Atkin's simple and ordinary lifestyle that presents the best way to appreciate his approach to judging. He formulated his ideas and wrote his judgments in a straightforward and accessible way; there was nothing ostentatious or oratorical about his judicial work. He relied on what he saw as common sense and fairness to reach decisions and frame arguments that would appeal to and convince the person on the street. He had no need for elaborate or indulgent excursions into philosophy or other academic pursuits. Although he believed that "law is a scientific subject," this did not mean that its analysis had to be esoteric or abstract. For Atkin, law was a *human* science and had to be understood as such. Indeed, Atkin devoted considerable effort to urging that the study of law be integrated into general education; he delivered many lectures to this effect and wrote the foreword for Edward Jenks's 1928 introductory text *The Book of English Law*. In 1934, he chaired the report of the Legal Education Committee, which gave legitimacy to the study of law as an academic as well as professional pursuit. Nevertheless, he urged that a distinction between the academic and professional study of law be maintained for the benefit of each.

Atkin's legal methodology was traditional and rigorous. In a style that ran in many ways against the casuistic origins and rule-bound operation of the common law, he believed that it was imperative to dig into the body of the accumulated case law and identify the more general principles that animated those rules. As he did in *Donoghue*, his quarrel with the dissenting Buckmaster was as much about the appropriate mode of judicial argument as it was about the actual outcome. Whereas Buckmaster refused to go beyond the discrete force of existing precedents, Atkin took a much more expansive and deductive approach. Not willing to take cases and rules at face value, he delved into the deeper reaches of the common law in search of its animating principles – "In English law there must be, and is, some general conception of relations giving rise to a duty of care, of which the particular cases found in the books are but instances." This offered a challenge to the prevailing orthodoxy. Although Atkin was not always successful in persuading his colleagues that this was a superior way of proceeding, he did set in motion a trend that soon became the accepted way of being a good judge. In this, he opened up a path (or, perhaps, rehabilitated a path that Lord Mansfield had cut but that had since become neglected) that many future judges would follow and regularize.

Yet, in adopting this principled approach, Atkin did not lose sight of the traditional values and ideals that supposedly energized the common law. Eschewing any doctrinaire politics or elite pretense, he put his methodology to work in the service of the ordinary person, especially the underdog. As an active member of the Protestant Church of Wales, he took seriously the duty to help those less well-off than himself. Although he was careful to respect the broader precedential force of the law, he directed it toward ends that were more liberal than traditional in substance: he was a friend to the wrongfully incarcerated, he protected the mentally ill, he was concerned about the safety of workers, he supported the victims of broken marriages in divorce reform (perhaps mindful of his mother's plight?), and he supported the use of tribunals to deal with war crimes. In all this, Lord Atkin was noble in the most enriching and basic spirit of the term.

To keep himself grounded, Atkin often called on the practical wisdom of his family and neighbors. Apart from maintaining good relations with his fellow bus travelers, he made a habit of using family mealtimes as a convenient occasion to sound out his ideas and impending decisions. At the family dining table, he would often tell his children of the cases that he was working on and seek their reaction. One evening, for example, he asked them about May Donoghue's case. Drawing on their Sunday School lessons, they responded by talking about the Parable of the Good Samaritan and its emphasis on how you should love your neighbor. Mulling this over in his chambers later, Lord Atkin is reputed to have worked up this casual reference into what is arguably still the leading judgment in the entire common law world – "The rule that you are to love your neighbour becomes in law, you must not injure your neighbour." Leavening the dry logic of the law with the earthy instincts of ordinary folk, Atkin did justice to both.

What made Lord Atkin into a great judge, therefore, was not a capacity to see what others could not see, but the ability to ensure that the law did not lose sight of the concerns and standpoint of ordinary people. As he stated in *Ambard v. Attorney General for Trinidad and Tobago* in 1936, "justice is not a cloistered virtue; she must be allowed to suffer the scrutiny and respectful, even though outspoken, comments of ordinary men." This is a rarer quality than many lawyers and judges care to admit. Of course, as well attuned as Atkin's radar was, he did not pander or play to the lowest common denominator. He wanted the law's doctrines, like the ordinary person, to live up to its own best ideals and self-image. For him, a person's neighbor was someone to be embraced, not kept at arm's length. He was not a disciple of the Frostian view that good fences make good neighbors.

Of course, none of this is to be taken to suggest that Atkin's judgments were somehow only his personal opinions outfitted in legalistic dress. Like other great judges, he

Photograph of Aberdovey, Wales, around the turn of the 20th century.
Source: Courtesy of www.oldukphotos.com.

saw his primary role to be that of a judge, not a politician
or policy analyst. But he reshaped what the most acceptable depiction of the judicial role was. With integrity and
consistency, he managed to create a distinctive approach to
judging that brought together an enviable grasp of law and
argumentative techniques at the same time as it utilized
them to advance a substantive agenda that was perceived
to arise from the best representation of that law itself. Neither adventurous nor cautious, Atkin hewed to a judicial
philosophy that put the common back into the common law
by legal means. In so doing, he made more friends than
he did enemies. R. W. Harding's observations on Atkin's

work in commercial law can be extended to his career more generally:

> It emerges how down-to-earth common sense, plus great clarity of thought, pervades all of his work. He isolates and states the central problem, and then brings out the facts surrounding it. And as he does it, somehow the solution seems to follow inevitably. This is the nature of his greatness, that when he indicates the answer, we wonder what mental blindness stopped us seeing from the beginning that it was the only feasible answer.

Considering his treatment by his fellow law lords after *Liversidge*, it is a genuine testament to his career not only that he was referenced as "one of the greatest common lawyers of this century," but also that he achieved that uncommon status by being both a judge's judge and a judicial reasonable man. Indeed, one of his detractors in *Liversidge*, the imposing Viscount Simon, was still minded to conclude that "his strength largely consisted in his conviction that English law is at bottom a sensible thing, and that, when he had grasped the facts and applied his great knowledge of the law to those facts, the conclusions would emerge."

Although almost all judges and lawyers found Atkin to be the model of professional courtesy and learning, he was not easily swayed in argument. Possessing a strong sense of right and wrong, he could be a prickly person to deal with once he had made up his mind (which he often did quickly and early). His decisiveness could be his weakness as much as his strength; it occasionally came across as righteousness and created the unfortunate impression that he was stubborn and intolerant. As Lord Denning later commented, "if he was against you, you could never get around him." But, by and large, there are few who have anything other than unstinting praise for this judge of acute intelligence and astute judgment.

Dick Atkin was a public servant in its fullest and most generous sense. By all accounts, he had a genuinely modest sense of himself and, like his grandmother, had little time for those who put on airs and graces. While sitting as a judge, he also accepted a number of important public assignments; he was chair of the Munitions Appeal Tribunal in 1916, chair of the Naturalisation of Aliens Committee in 1918, chair of the War Cabinet Committee on Women in Industry in 1918, and chair of the Irish Deportees Compensation Tribunal in 1924. He undertook these responsibilities with characteristic conscientiousness and skill. As well as being president of the Medico-Legal Society from 1923 to 1927, he assumed the important chairmanship of the Judicial Enquiry into Crime and Insanity in the mid-1920s; he made recommendations, considered harsh by today's standards (because he was also in favor of capital and corporal punishment generally), about how the law should deal with afflicted criminals. On top of all this, he was on the Council of the University College of Wales, Aberystwyth, and a governor of both his old school,

Christ College, and Charterhouse School. Taken together, these commitments say much about his public-spiritedness and his willingness to give back to society; he walked the walk as well as talked the talk of *Liversidge*.

One of Atkin's last undertakings was to advocate for the establishment of a war crimes tribunal to punish the Nazi leaders. He did this not to exact revenge but to vindicate civilized values. In February 1944, he was seconded to the War Crimes Committee on Means of Enforcement. Adopting a predictable line of argument, he urged that a separate and independent court would be needed if national prejudices were to be contained. He was adamant that all trials must be conducted strictly in line with agreed legal standards, before specially trained judges, and with a representative from the country of the alleged victims. Unfortunately, Atkin would not live to see the promulgation of the London Charter of the International Military Tribunal (or Nuremberg Charter) in August 1945. But it was somehow fitting that his last major accomplishment should be on behalf of his country of birth, Australia, as he was their designated representative on the committee; it rounded out his life in a neat and timely way.

A few months after his committee work and while still an active judge in the House of Lords, Atkin contracted bronchitis. As an ailing, old, and widowed man (Lizzie had died a few years earlier) of seventy-six, he went into a quick decline and died on 25 June 1944. It was some comfort to him and his grown family that he spent his last few days in his home of Craig-y-Don in Aberdyfi. He was buried there with little pomp in the local churchyard. It had been a long but fulfilling journey from tropical northern Queensland to the more equable hills of Merionydd. He had done even more than his mother, father, or grandmother could have wished for him. Apart from his life peerage, he had accumulated many honors – he became an honorary Fellow of Magdalen College and the British Academy, and he received honorary degrees from Oxford, Cambridge, Reading, and London. Yet, true to his modest beginnings, he would have been particularly grateful for the fact that he is most fondly remembered as a good man; being commemorated as a great judge would have been so much frippery to him. In his case, the formal title of "lord appeal *in ordinary*" was true in both style and substance.

6

Tom Denning

An English Gardener

Like so many others, the relationship between law and justice is complicated and confusing. Although we tend to think of courts as being involved in the administration of justice, the role and responsibilities of judges are far from straightforward in fulfilling that task. Indeed, legal commentators diverge considerably in their opinions about the extent to which justice and law can march along different paths and with different destinations. In negotiating this central, if troubling, terrain, judges reveal much about the law and themselves.

For some, the role of the judge is simply to apply the law as it is; this in itself will result in justice being done. The fact that this may lead to a certain injustice in particular and discrete cases is considered to be the price to be paid for a legal process that recommends certainty and predictability as overarching virtues. Subscribing to the conventional wisdom of Baron Rolfe's adage that "hard cases are apt to introduce bad law," such proponents maintain that bending the law to meet difficult or obscure facts is ultimately more trouble than it is worth. Others, of course, take a different tack. They insist that the primary duty of judges is to do justice and that the maintenance of legal clarity is not weighty enough to defeat the delivery of justice in individual cases. The law will lose respect and place even greater distance between itself and people if it fails to deliver justice.

Lord Denning was decidedly one of the judges who thought that justice must be done. Judges were justices, not simply a special kind of lawyer. With a characteristic defiance and stubbornness, he was prepared to be as creative as possible in locating and applying law so as to achieve justice: "There is always a way round. There is always an option – in my philosophy – by which justice can be done." Indeed, the hallmark of his long career was his single-minded quest to bend the law to his own philosophy and sense of justice. It was this contested quality that made him not only a great judge but also a controversial judge. His influence obliged supporters and detractors alike to confront in stark terms the compelling questions of much jurisprudential inquiry – why should substantive justice trump legal right? Why should one judge's view of justice prevail over that of other judges or people generally? If not law's justice, then whose?

If ever there were to be a life that characterized the twentieth century, it would be that of Alfred Thompson ("Tom") Denning. He was born in the last year of the nineteenth century and died in the last year of the twentieth century. In the intervening one hundred years, he managed to compile a career that illustrated how much times changed in England from the Victorian era through the Swinging Sixties to the Internet Age. For good and bad, Tom Denning's professional and personal life tracks the quickening and uneven trajectory of the modern age.

He was born prematurely on 23 January 1899 on Newbury Street in Whitchurch, Hampshire, which is to the southwest of London. His parents, Charles and Clara, ran a local draper's shop. He was the fifth in a family of six, with five brothers and one sister, and was likely his mother's favorite; he was named by his sister Marjorie after Alfred the Great and took his mother's maiden name of Thompson. Never a robust child, he was nicknamed Tom Thumb. Family was to be a strong force in his life; it offered security, continuity, and settled values. Two brothers died in the First World War; his eldest brother, Jack, succumbed to shrapnel wounds in a 1916 assault, and his older brother Gordon died at home in May 1918 from tuberculosis acquired during combat. These tragic losses led to financial troubles as well as personal grief for the family. His older brother Reginald became an army general, and his younger brother, Norman, became a navy admiral; both were knighted. Although from humble roots, it was a family of great achievement and public service.

Denning's own war service came at the end of his first year at university. After attending Andover Grammar School, he took a scholarship place at Magdalen College, Oxford, studying mathematics; he had taught himself Greek to gain admission. He enlisted as part of the national draft soon after his eighteenth birthday and saw action in France. At the end of the war in November 1918, he was recovering from influenza in a military hospital in France. By the next February, he was fit enough to return to Oxford and complete his studies. However, as with so many of that generation, these tragedies left their mark on Denning, who dedicated himself to making good on the sacrifices of this lost "breed of mighty men" and his own good fortune of making it relatively unscathed through those harrowing experiences. Like Holmes (Chapter 4), Denning's sense of himself and his need to contribute to society were marked by this crucial episode.

Always an exceptional student, Denning taught mathematics at Winchester College, Oxford, for a year after his graduation (as well as geology, which he had never studied before). However, being less than enamored with an academic's life and inspired by a visit to Winchester Assizes, he returned to Magdalen in 1921 to complete his legal studies and began his self-confessed love affair with the law. By the next year, he had already finished his legal education with a first-class degree. Indeed, throughout his life, one of his startling features was that he did things not only to the very highest standards but also in very short order; his whole career proceeded with unrivaled achievement and alacrity.

As all aspiring barristers must do, Denning joined one of the Inns of Court, in his case Lincoln's Inn. He was called to the bar in June 1923 at the top of his class. He secured chambers at 4 Brick Court in the Temple. However, even with a prize studentship to his credit, he spent his first year or so "briefless" and wrote pleadings and opinions without being paid. Like all fledgling barristers (who could share chambers but could not be in partnership with other barristers) in this most elite of professions, he had to earn his spurs before he was able to attract paying clients. But this he did, and, by 1927, he had begun to establish a solid and successful general practice with some specialization in railway litigation. During these years, he also performed the prodigious task of editing *Smith's Leading Cases*, a widely relied-on professional compendium, and learned, as he put it, "most of the law I ever knew." This undertaking was the basis of his enviable and mostly reliable memory for cases and their facts; it was a talent that served him well, even if it irked some counsel before him, in deciding cases on precedents that had not been pleaded or placed before him.

As his career developed on its inevitable arc of increasing success, Denning's personal life established itself. In December 1932, he married Mary Harvey, a local vicar's daughter; they had been courting for almost ten years, but marriage had been delayed for reasons of social convention and Mary's ill health. His only child, Robert, was born in August 1938, a few months after Denning had become a very young king's counsel (a status conferred on only the most able and senior barristers) on April Fools' Day. Robert followed in his father's footsteps, but as a scientist, not a lawyer. He went on to have a very celebrated career as a professor of inorganic chemistry at Denning's old Oxford college, Magdalen.

However, Denning's family life was blighted by the death of Mary in late November 1941. Since the beginning of the Second World War, at which point Denning was not young enough for active service, he had lived with Mary and Robert in the Sussex village of Cuckfield. Although this part of southern England was a bomb alley during the war, Denning loved the traditional pastoral life and, when not acting as a legal advisor to the government in London or Leeds, spent as much time as he could there. This was a pattern that he continued for the rest of his life, buying a property, the Lawn, in 1960 in Whitchurch, near his old childhood home. He lived there until his death with his second wife, a widow named Joan Stuart (and her three children), whom he had married after a brief courtship in 1945 and who died in 1992.

During the war, at the decidedly young age of forty-four, Denning was to take up his first official role in a judicial career that would last almost a further forty years. In December 1943, he was appointed a Commissioner of Assize. This proved to be a trial run for his elevation to the full bench and, in March 1944, he became a High Court judge in the Probate, Divorce and Admiralty Division and later, in 1945, in the King's Bench Division. In his four short years at the high court, he began to make his mark and set a trend of standing on the side of the "little man." It was during this time that he rendered his perhaps most famous decision in the *High Trees House* case. By late 1948, he had been made a member of the Court of Appeal, where he sat for nine years and continued his mission to leave his own stamp on the law's development. In 1957, he became a law lord and a member of (at that time) the United Kingdom's highest appellate court, the Judicial Committee of the House of Lords; he took the title of Lord Denning of Whitchurch and sat, as was customary, as both a judge and a legislator in that upper assembly of Parliament.

For many lawyers and judges, this conferral of a law lordship would have marked the crowning glory of an already illustrious career. However, Denning was no ordinary judge and no ordinary person. If greatness is as much about changing the rules as playing well by them, then Denning was in a class of his own. He was disillusioned by the fact that, in the House of Lords, he sat as a member of a panel of five judges and therefore could not have the kind of impact on the law's development that he desired. When the position of Master of the Rolls, the presiding judge of the Court of Appeal's Civil Division, became vacant, Denning decided that this was a more suitable role. Not only would he be one among three sitting judges on each case, but also he would have the power to determine with which two fellow judges he would sit. This was an opportunity not to be missed and, in April 1962, he became Master of the Rolls. Although he sought to protect the values of the little man, he wanted to do so as a big man.

For the next twenty years, Denning continued his judicial mission. With a summer interlude to head the Profumo Inquiry (a call girl scandal involving a cabinet minister) in the summer of 1963 for which he became a temporary public celebrity, he utilized his powerful post to leave a lasting impression on the common law. His often cavalier use and, where convenient, disregard of precedent made as many foes as friends. His decisions were regularly overturned by the House of Lords. However, because his views were often in line with popular sentiments, Parliament occasionally came to his aid by enacting legislation in line with his decisions. An anecdote by John Donaldson, Denning's successor as Master of the Rolls, says much. After an appeal, Denning said, "Well John, we're allowing the appeal, aren't we?" Donaldson said, "No, Tom, we are not." "Fine," said Denning. Then he said to the other judge, "We're allowing the appeal,

The Denning family's drapery shop on Newbury Street, Whitchurch, c. 1910. *Source:* Hampshire Record Office: TOP338/2/10.

aren't we?" "No, Tom, we are not," he replied. "Right," said Denning, with a big beaming smile and no rancor whatsoever, "You two will have to dissent."

Denning's reception among the legal and academic chattering classes ran from mostly fawning admiration to occasional vehement opposition. But, love or loathe him, he was his own man. There was and remains the view that Denning was a legal force of nature. No account of English and Commonwealth twentieth-century law is complete without his dominant presence; he often set the terms of debate, even if he did not always carry the day in every particular instance.

His claim to be counted in the pantheon of great judges is almost without serious challenge. But the assessment about whether his overall influence on the law was for good or ill is another matter entirely.

By any standards, Denning was a singular individual. But, like many colorful characters, he had a monochromatic view of the world. His clarity of vision was both his great strength and his weakness. In particular, he had a marked tendency to see people and values in black and white; there were very few shades of grey in his philosophy or approach. Having the audacious courage of his own settled convictions, he rarely second-guessed himself or exhibited any qualms about what it meant to do the right thing on particular facts or in particular circumstances: "If there is any rule of law which impairs the doing of justice, then it is the province of the judge to do all he legitimately can to avoid that rule – or even to change it – so as to do justice in the instant case before him." This was both the guarantor of his greatness and the harbinger of his downfall. When you have a set of values that were forged in the early Edwardian years of the twentieth century, it is not surprising that you might face some difficulties and arouse some opposition in applying them in the second half of such a rapidly changing century. This was even more the case if those values had a distinctly pastoral or traditional mien to them, as Denning's did.

As he had shown in his education, one of Denning's sterling qualities was not simply his undoubted intelligence but his quickness of thought and delivery. In the same way that he had sped through his education and early apprenticeship as a barrister, he was the very model of an attentive and timely judge. He listened patiently to those appearing before him. But, once he had made up his mind (which was often very early in the proceedings), he acted with a direct and decisive swiftness. However, when combined with his rather two-dimensional grasp of the changing modern world, this speediness could often run to hastiness, with its accompanying tendency to forego reflection and second thought. Denning seemed to have almost never experienced any of the indecision or procrastination that bedevils and occasionally rescues lesser mortals.

One of the points of contention about Denning's judgments was his writing style. Reflecting his general character, he was a simple and straightforward stylist. This, in part, was driven by his exemplary belief that, if ordinary citizens were to appreciate and respect the law, it was imperative that they understand the courts' judgments if they bothered to read them. He made a conscious and concerted effort to shun a cold or clinical technique and, instead, cultivated a more colorful and colloquial style. Whereas some saw his judgments as showcasing the spare and sinewy style of a Hemingway, others caricatured his efforts as resembling the breathless prose of the Hardy Boys. What can be agreed is that these narratives were instantly recognizable. Some of the more memorable of his self-confessed "judgments as short stories" are as follows:

Old Peter Beswick was a coal merchant in Eccles, Lancashire. He had no business premises. All he had was a lorry, scales and weights. He used to take the lorry to the yard of the National Coal Board, where he bagged coal and took it round to his customers in the neighborhood. His nephew, John Joseph Beswick, helped him in the business. . . .

It happened on 19 April 1964. It was bluebell-time in Kent. Mr. And Mrs. Hinz had been married some ten years, and they had four children, all aged nine and under. The youngest was one. Mrs. Hinz was a remarkable woman. In addition to her own four, she was foster-mother to four other children. To add to it, she was two months pregnant with her fifth child. . . .

Broadchalke is one of the most pleasing villages in England. Old Herbert Bundy was a farmer there. His home was at Yew Tree Farm. It went back for 300 years. His family had been there for generations. It was his only asset. But he did a very foolish thing. He mortgaged it to the bank. Up to the very hilt. Not to borrow money for himself, but for the sake of his son. Now the bank have come down on him. They have foreclosed. . . .

This is the case of the Birmingham bombers. Thursday, 21 November 1974. Eight minutes past eight in the evening. The telephone rang in a newspaper office in Birmingham.

A young man picked it up. It was from a call-box. "Is that 'The Birmingham Post'?" asked a voice with an Irish accent. "Yes." The voice went on: "There is a bomb planted at the Rotunda. There is another in New Street near the Tax Office." That was all. At once the young man dialed the police. He repeated the message to them. The police were quick as lightning. Their cars rushed to those addresses – screeching their way. But they were too late. The bombs went off before the police could get there. Each in a crowded public house. One in The Mulberry Bush. The other in The Tavern in the Town. Both were devastated. Dead and dying lay everywhere. Twenty-one people were killed and 161 injured.

A large part of Denning's appeal was that he was a baffling mix of the traditional and the irreverent that defies easy categorization. Although many students of the law tend to glorify Denning as an iconoclast who was a liberal trailblazer, he was almost reactionary and progressive in equal measure. For example, as much as he revered the law as an embodiment of English common sense, he was not one of those traditionalists who maintained that the common law runs from time immemorial, as some lawyers are wont to pretend. He was clearly of the view, which he put into action daily, that judges develop and nurture the law much like a garden over the years; they plant some new blooms here and a few new shrubs there and often weed out the old brush where necessary. Indeed, as emphasized by several commentators, this understanding of the common law as an English garden was a constant refrain in his approach to law and life – he believed in the organic and communal quality of the true England as a blessed community in which each could be, as Kipling put it, "a partner in the Glory of the Garden." This bucolic nostalgia proved to be both his peculiar calling card and the cause of his startling downfall.

Under such a guiding philosophy, Denning stood by his guns and refused to distinguish or finesse earlier decisions on technical grounds. He was nothing if not direct. If an established precedent got in the way of justice, he would walk right over it rather than take some circuitous or subtle route to avoid it. This did not endear him to many of his judicial colleagues. However, as in other matters, he was a man ahead of his time. Denning had long advocated that the House of Lords should not be bound by its own decisions; the House accepted this position a number of years after he left, with its Practice Statement of 1966. However, he locked horns with the law lords over whether or not the Court of Appeal was bound to follow its own past decisions. In 1969 in *Gallie v. Lee*, a contract case about the circumstances in which persons can escape the effect of documents that they have signed, Denning held that the court was not bound by its own past decisions ("or, at any rate, not absolutely bound"). He could not stomach the idea that technical formalities could stand in the way of substantive justice. Yet, this cavalier approach stood in sharp contrast to his unbending attachment to more traditional values. After all, in *Gallie* itself, he found against a deserving defendant who was bound by the effects of a document she had signed but not understood.

A couple of years later in *Broome v. Cassell*, a defamation case, Denning even went so far as to suggest that, when a precedent set by the House of Lords had been doubted in the Commonwealth and other common law jurisdictions, it might be ignored by lower courts. Although the House of Lords upheld the Court of Appeal's decision, it made it clear that Denning or any other appellate judge did not have the authority to reject the precedent of the House. As Lord Hailsham rather tartly put it, "the fact is, and I hope it will never be necessary to say so again, that in the hierarchical system of courts which exists in this country, it is necessary for each lower tier, including the Court of Appeal, to accept loyally the decisions of the higher tiers." Throughout the 1970s, Denning continued to expand the circumstances in which Court of Appeal judges might exercise their discretion to deviate from earlier and otherwise binding precedents.

In taking this approach, Denning placed great stock in the independence of the judiciary. He contended that judges stand "between the individual and the state, protecting the individual from any interference with his freedom which is not justified by the law." And, in many judgments, he followed through on this commitment. In case after case, he resisted executive claims to being able to exercise unfettered discretion and insisted that administrative officers and even cabinet ministers must be held accountable by being obliged

Lord Denning, Master of the Rolls. Photograph by Bernard Lee Schwartz, 1977. *Source:* © National Portrait Gallery, London. http://www.npg.org.uk.

to act fairly and reasonably. Yet, for all his suspicion about power's abuse and his support for the little man, it was deeply ironic that Denning saw no problem with his own unchecked and unaccountable power as a judge who, after all, was only a privileged government bureaucrat. He simply concluded that "every Judge on his appointment discards all politics and all prejudices. Someone must be trusted. Let it be the Judges." This hardly passes muster as a convincing reassurance.

Denning was no fan of legislation. He saw it as a distinctly second-best source of law. Antagonistic to systematic or overarching theories of justice, he was much more concerned with the facts of the case before him and the fate of the flesh-and-blood litigants. Doing justice in individual cases trumped any concern about implementing more general schemes of social policy; litigants were not to be dispatched as victims to ideological purity. Accordingly, notwithstanding its democratic origins, statute law was treated as being inferior to the common law in authority and wisdom. He showed little compunction in reading legislative enactments against the continuing force of the common law's general principles, which, of course, were to be identified and elucidated by judges like him. He pioneered a purposive and gap-filling approach to statutory interpretation, which, although initially resisted by the House of Lords, was later adopted, albeit in a more modest form.

Denning's general approach to judging (and to other unlike-minded judges) was neatly encapsulated in one of his dissenting judgments in his first stint on the Court of Appeal. In the 1951 case of *Candler*, he had to decide on whether to extend negligence liability, which was first introduced by Lord Atkin (see Chapter 5) in 1932 in *Donoghue v. Stevenson* for defective products, to the making of statements by professionals. In a sweeping judgment, Denning surveyed existing precedent and declared that "the novelty of the action" should not be a bar to allowing the appeal and imposing liability. He divided judges into two camps in confronting such situations: "On the one side there were the timorous souls who were fearful of allowing a new cause of action. On the other side there were the bold spirits who were ready to allow it if justice so required." Although this categorization did not go down too well with his more "timorous" colleagues, it did capture Denning's own sense of his bold and spirited approach to judging. He saw himself as a kind of judicial Captain Kirk who would "boldly go" where others were too fearful to tread; he seemed to believe that he had a special dispensation to pursue a personal calling of just lawmaking. In this instance, Denning's prescience was vindicated in 1963 when the House of Lords in *Hedley Byrne* established a doctrinal framework for liability for professional misstatements that owed much to Denning's earlier judgment.

Near the end of his judicial career, Denning became even more impatient at the law's resistance to change and its hewing to technical precedents. Picking up on a theme that he had run for several years, in 1981 in *Lamb v. London Borough of Camden*, he sailed close to a very radical view of law's development and the judicial role. He opined that various doctrinal rules were little more than "devices" to answer larger "policy" questions about the appropriate range and extent of legal liability. Quoting his own words from an earlier case, he noted "the time has come when, in cases of new import, we should decide them according to the reason of the thing." Rather than conceal this task behind technical issues and evasions, "judges [should] openly ask themselves the question: what is the best policy for the law to adopt?" This was a very bold move and, some would argue, a step too far. If the law was really about social policy, what made the judges capable or trustworthy in addressing those matters with competence or confidence? If law was really about policy, why should lawyers be entrusted with its resolution and development?

It is not surprising that, with his heavy and self-assured touch, Denning did not endear himself to all his colleagues or commentators generally. He had a long-running contretemps with Viscount Simonds, who sat in the House of Lords from 1945 to 1962 and was Lord Chancellor, the head of the judiciary, and effectively Denning's boss, from 1951 to 1954. Sharing a luke-cool personal relationship, Denning and Simonds had very different views about a judge's role and responsibilities. Simonds often took pains to point out Denning's failings in his judgments. In the *Magor* case about statutory interpretation, he chastised Denning for recommending an approach that "appears to be a naked usurpation of the legislative function under the thin disguise of interpretation." Again, in the *Howell* case of 1951, in distancing his own judgment from that of Denning, Simonds rebuked Denning by stating, "My Lords, I know of no such principle in our law, nor was any authority for it cited." Within the polite discourse of English judicial pronouncements, these were cutting words. Of course, by labeling many of his brethren (for they were all men) as timorous souls, Denning managed to get their collective backs up.

For instance, in *Candler*, Lord Justice Asquith captured the mood of many when he ended his own judgment somewhat sardonically by saying that "if this relegates me to the company of 'timorous souls,' I must face that consequence with such fortitude as I can command." In short, with his almost set-in-stone sense of what was right and his direct manner, Denning was both his own best and worst advocate.

When Denning was appointed to the House of Lords, he received, as was customary, a life peerage. He took the title of Baron Denning of Whitchurch. But, most revealingly, the motto on his coat of arms was *fiat justitia* – "Let justice be done." This was an abbreviation of the more well-known maxim from Lord Mansfield (see Chapter 2), *fiat justitia, ruat caelum* – "Let justice be done, though the heavens should fall." With his typical mix of mischievousness and single-mindedness, Denning left off the second part of the phrase because he insisted that, if justice was done, there was no way that the heavens could in fact fall. This attenuated motto and Denning's explanation for it offer clear glimpses at his broader approach to law and justice. There was a definite connection not only between justice and law but also between justice and a heavenly wisdom. At least, that is, when each was viewed through Denning's own rather shuttered and unclouded vision of Christian virtue. To understand and appreciate Denning, therefore, it is obligatory to have a genuine grasp of his sense of justice.

Denning was not a great intellectual theorizer or system-atizer. His sense of justice grew out of his early upbringing and his lifelong commitment to Christianity in its Anglican form, not from any textbook learning or extended study. For him, justice was a natural instinct that was reinforced by his religious faith. In a speech in Nairobi in 1973, he opined that "the nearest we can get to defining justice is to say that it is what the right-minded members of the community – those who have the right spirit within them – believe to be fair." It goes without saying that Denning never doubted that he had that "right spirit." Of course, the fact that the English judiciary and the Church of England had traditionally been fellow travelers meant that Denning's conscience was very much in tune with that of the legal and social establishment. As the homogeneity of English society began to change in the mid-twentieth century, this customary sense of fairness began to fragment and was revealed as the rather partial and parochial set of values that it always had been.

The particular substance of those values cut in varied directions. In Denning's understanding of society, he clearly envisaged a natural order of rank and role in which each person, high and low, was both comforted and confined. This is particularly so in his attitude to women. All the women in his life – his mother, sister (who gets scant mention in his family biography), and his two wives – were revered but seen exclusively as helpmates for the grander exploits of the men in their lives. Although Denning is deservedly celebrated for his groundbreaking introduction of the deserted wives' equity doctrine, it very much fit with his traditional acceptance of the role of the husband and wife as a family unit rather than with any more progressive notion of modern feminism. This was a doctrinal battle that he waged all though his judicial career. From 1947 and on after the Matrimonial Proceedings and Property Act of 1970, he insisted wives acquired an equitable but legally enforceable right in the matrimonial home against their husbands. He never wavered in this commitment, despite some legislative setbacks and regular rebuttal by the House of Lords. Whatever his motivation, it was a standout triumph that reflected his doggedness as well as his sense of right and wrong.

Nevertheless, these widely acclaimed achievements must be leavened somewhat by other less stellar examples of his treatment of women. In the case of *Ward* in 1971, Denning had to decide on the procedural merits of a young woman's expulsion from a teacher's training college. In an otherwise measured and professional judgment, the Master of the Rolls suddenly offered a most revealing aside:

> She had broken the rules most flagrantly. Instead of going into lodgings, she had this man with her, night after night, in the Hall of Residence where such a thing was absolutely forbidden. That is a fine example to set to others! And she a girl training to be a teacher! I expect the Governors and the Staff all thought that she was quite an unsuitable person for it. She would never make a teacher. No parent would knowingly entrust their child to her care.

Yet there can be no doubting Denning's genuine commitment to ensuring that the little man was protected by the courts from overbearing institutions or elites. Of course, even this was based not on any grandly egalitarian theory, but on his own traditional sense of noblesse oblige; it was what endeared him to many and often persuaded some, wrongly, to embrace him as a modern liberal or progressive. In case after case, he refused to adhere to the charms of freedom of contract. In *Lloyds Bank* in 1975 (and in contrast to *Gallie*), he protected "poor old Mr. Bundy" (as the trial judge put it) against the heavy bargaining hand of the bank. But perhaps his most significant intervention was in the *High Trees House* case at the very beginning of his judicial career in 1947; this is still a great case that all law students must know and through which many are first introduced to Denning.

A landlord had promised to halve the amount of rent while London was being bombed during the war and while the tenants (who were subject to ninety-nine-year leases) had left London. On their return, the landlord wanted the full amount. As the leases stipulated a set amount and as there was only a bare promise without any "consideration" (i.e., a giving of something of value, usually money, that turns a bare promise into a legal agreement), which was technically necessary to make a promise part of a binding agreement, the landlord had an apparently valid legal claim for the full amount based on the original lease. In a truly bold and adventurous decision, Denning introduced the

Lord Denning at home in his garden, aged 97. Photograph by Tim Ockenden, 1996. *Source:* Press Association Images.

doctrine of "equitable estoppel." Relying in part on some obscure precedents that he had unearthed in his earlier editorial work on *Smith's Leading Cases*, he insisted, "the time has now come for the validity of such a promise to be recognised." A person who reasonably relied on a promise made within an existing contractual relationship could not be denied or "estopped" from relying on that promise against its maker, even though there was no consideration. Although there was much initial resistance to this innovation, it has become accepted as an indispensable equitable addition to the law's body of guiding principles.

Throughout his career, Denning was fearless and some might say wanton in his willingness to challenge what he considered to be wrongheaded or ill-conceived precedents.

He was not always successful at his first shot, but he more often than not managed to persuade his judicial colleagues that his novel intervention was worth a try. This was a result of his uncanny capacity for cogent arguments as well as the common sense of his views. After all, most of the judges were cut from similar traditional English cloth as Denning himself. He may have represented those customary values and an approach to law in a style that was more uncompromising than theirs, but his values and approach were shared by the judiciary. At least, that is, at midcentury. However, unfortunately or not, those very same values that served him so well became a liability as the years moved on and the country began to change in its social stance and makeup.

As Denning had been appointed to the bench before the introduction of a mandatory retirement age, his judicial tenure was unaffected by his seventy-fifth birthday. He was maintaining the same pace and practice in his eightieth year as he had done in the early years of his career. He conceded that he had "every Christian virtue except resignation." However, by 1982, he was getting not only long in the tooth but also a little too cavalier in his willingness to share his opinions on social matters, great and small. He had lived through the 1960s and 1970s, but he had not really warmed to, let alone caught, these decades' challenging spirit. He was still very much the character or caricature of an

Edwardian gentleman. If anything, his views had hardened, and he had become less concerned to be discrete or deferential about them.

In the *Dowell Lea* case in early 1982, Denning rendered one of his few legalistic decisions. He refused to find that Sikhs were protected as a "race" under the existing discrimination law; a young boy had been sent home from school because he and his parents refused to remove his turban. Denning took the impolitic line that "you must remember that it is perfectly lawful to discriminate against [Roman Catholics, communists, hippies, moonies, or skinheads] to whom you object – so long as they are not a racial group." This went squarely against Parliament's expressed intentions, and his decision was overturned by the House of Lords. Also, in 1980, he had played a less than honorable role in the Birmingham Six case of *McIlkenny*, in which he dismissed efforts by the convicted bombers to sue the police for abuses in pretrial custody. The problem was less his decision and more the fact that he took to his bully pulpit and ranted that

> this case shows what a civilized country we are. Here are six men who have been convicted of the most wicked murder of 21 innocent people. They are guilty of gross perjury. Yet the state continued to lavish huge sums on them in their actions against the police. It is high time that it stopped. It is really an attempt to set aside the convictions by sidewind. It is a scandal that should not be allowed to continue.

It was later established unequivocally that the Birmingham Six had been set up by the police, that their confessions had been coerced, and that they had no part in the bombings.

In addition to still hearing a full roster of appeals and delivering more than his fair share of judgments (and regularly being reproved by the House of Lords), Denning had also taken to publishing a variety of extrajudicial musings and recollections. Having finished *The Family Story* in 1981, he followed it with *What Next in the Law* in 1982. This was intended to be a kind of expansive glossary to his mounting list of decided cases and to demonstrate how, in Denning's rather dated view of the world, "the experience of the past points the way to the future." This seemed a dubious project in its general ambition and proved to be disastrous in its detailed performance.

Always a supporter of tighter immigration laws, Denning made the forceful argument that not all members of the English community had the same standards of justice, and, in particular, he called into question the suitability of some immigrants and nonwhites for jury duty. He incorporated remarks, later shown to be false, he had made a year earlier on the occasion of the Bristol Race Riots that the black defendants' lawyers had made their jury selections and objections based on race. In *What Next in the Law*, he wrote that

[t]he English are no longer a homogenous race. They are white and black, coloured and brown. They no longer

share the same standards of conduct. Some of them come from countries where bribery and graft are accepted as an integral part of life: and where stealing is a virtue so long as you are not found out. They no longer share the same code of morals. They no longer share the same religious beliefs. They no longer share the same respect for the law.

By any standards, this was foolish stuff. But for such a prominent and powerful member of the judiciary to have such ideas, let alone share them widely, was tantamount to professional suicide. Indeed, the fact that Denning somehow thought that such views might be acceptable only testified to how much he had become out of step with the times. There was the anticipated public outcry, particularly from black barristers. With his integrity compromised, Denning quickly made the decision to retire; the book was withdrawn from print and the offending sections excised. It was a sad, if not entirely unexpected, denouement to such a singular career. And it provided a signal example of what can happen to those who linger on beyond their putative sell-by date.

There was a sense of general relief within the legal and judicial community that Denning had made the decision to retire. Tributes poured in: he was praised as being a judge of immense and unmatched gifts who had left an indelible mark on his beloved common law. But it was left to Rudy Narayan of the Society of Black Lawyers to offer the most elegant and telling footnote to an illustrious if contestable career:

> Lord Denning remains one of the greatest judicial minds of this century. A great judge has erred greatly in the intellectual loneliness of advanced years; while his remarks should be rejected and rebutted he is yet, in a personal way, entitled to draw on that reservoir of community regard which he has in many quarters and to seek understanding, if not forgiveness.

As an active judge of thirty-eight years, Lord Denning had set a record for judicial service that is unlikely to be bettered now that there is a mandatory retirement age. But there was more to Denning than staying power. He had managed to set a new standard of what it meant to be a "bold spirit" and resist the strong forces in play to toe the prevailing judicial line. Although his particular decisions and their informing values might not always be worth preserving, he changed received views about what was involved in the art of judging. He gave the judicial craft a very different twist.

Although Denning offered to retire immediately, he was persuaded to stay on until the end of the legal term. He delivered his final judgment on 29 September 1982 in the *George Mitchell* case. Fittingly, he gave an exemplary judgment that showcased much that was best about him. The plaintiff farmers purchased cabbage seeds from the defendant merchants. There was an exclusion clause, printed on the back of the invoice, that limited all liability to the cost of the seeds. The plaintiffs were not aware of this clause. Whereas the seeds cost £192, the farmers suffered losses of more than £60,000 when the harvest failed due to the poor quality of the seeds. According to the Sale of Goods Act, such exclusion clauses could only be relied on to the extent that it was "fair and reasonable" to do so. Denning reasoned that it would not be fair and reasonable to allow reliance on the exclusion clause and agreed with the trial judge's damages award of £100,000. In his judgment (which he begins, courtesy of Lewis Carroll's *Through the Looking Glass*, with "'The time has come,' the Walrus said, 'to talk of many things – of ships and shoes and sealing wax – of cabbages and kings'"), he offered a convenient and elegant sweep through some of his favorite legal themes on "freedom of contract" (the unequal bargaining power between the parties); the "serious negligence" of the merchants; the farmers' inability to learn that the seeds were defective; and the lack of available insurance for the buyer but not the seller. It was a fitting and relatively low-key formal end to a distinguished judicial career.

If there is any validity to the humorous line that old judges don't die, they simply lose their appeal, then it rings true for Denning. After the ignominy of his sudden departure from the bench, it might reasonably be assumed that he would have learned his lesson and, to be blunt, have kept his mouth shut. But, in 1990, he gave an ill-advised interview to A. N. Wilson, a noted columnist, for the *Spectator* magazine. By then a nonagenarian, he roamed and ranted freely about the demise of good old-fashioned values. He repeated his complaint that "all the words in the language which we used to condemn immorality of any description have been taken out – no bastards, no buggers." In addition to continuing to condemn homosexuality as an "unnatural vice" that undermines "the integrity of the human race," he objected to the influx of European law into England; he referred erroneously to Sir Leon Brittan, a former cabinet minister and then European commissioner, as a "German Jew, telling us what to do with our English law." Denning rounded off this harangue by observing about the recently exonerated Guilford Four (alleged IRA bombers) that "they'd probably have hanged the right men – not proved against them, that's all."

Some, like A. N. Wilson, lament the fact that Denning had lived to too old an age or, at least, had stayed in the public eye too long. If he had died at around seventy, it was argued, his "unblemished reputation as one of the great libertarians of English history" would have been safe and secured. Although there is some merit to this view, it misses something profound and telling about Tom Denning. It was not that he acquired his objectionable views late in life, but that he had always held them; they simply bubbled to the surface in his later years. To fully understand and appreciate Denning's life and legacy is to incorporate these essential, not aberrational, if objectionable elements of his personal philosophy. Without them, there is only an incomplete and hagiographic portrait of Tom Denning. His claim to greatness is that his warts and all detract from his attractiveness but not from his influence. Although he might have leavened his general boldness with some occasional timorousness, Denning was a great judge both because of *and* despite his foibles and flaws.

Lord Denning died on 5 March 1999, a few months past his one hundredth birthday. He had assembled a life and career of truly Churchillian dimensions. Like Winston, he was a larger-than-life character. Not only did he leave his own distinctive mark on all that he did and tend to overwhelm the contribution of others, but also his reception was far from uniform or uncontroversial. Although most would place both characters in the great category, some would be more begrudging than others in their evaluations. Like Churchill, Denning had good and bad phases in his long judicial career. In contrast to Churchill, the heights of his early judicial decisions were offset by the lows of his later fumbles. Yet Denning also fulfilled a huge role as "a partner in the Glory of the Garden." Not only did he tend law's shrubs and plants with true devotion and unceasing care, but he changed people's understanding of what the "glory" of that garden can be. He gardened for England with everything, good and bad, that this implies.

7

Thurgood Marshall

A Man on a Mission

Many people want their heroes to be straightforward and simple figures. Reduced to almost cardboard cutouts, they become as much mythic caricatures as real-life characters; there is little room for nuance or contradiction in the composition. However, heroes are often ordinary people who are placed or find themselves in extraordinary circumstances. Behind the myth, there is a flesh-and-blood individual who is as or even more complex than most others. Indeed, some heroes build their claim to greatness around their experience as and empathy with the lives of ordinary people (like Lord Atkin, Chapter 5). The hallmark of their heroic status is to be found in the fact that they rise above but never forget their own ordinary existence; they scale the ladder of success, not to escape their ordinary lives, but with the avowed ambition of taking other ordinary people along with them on the climb.

As resilient as he was resourceful, Thurgood Marshall was one such judge. He put his ordinary experience to extraordinary effect; he negotiated that perilous territory between celebrity and greatness. As talented as he was, he never forgot who he was, because, as an African American, he was never allowed to forget. Nor did he want to forget – "There are only two things I *have to* do – stay black and die." No matter what he achieved or how high he rose, he would always be seen, for both better and worse, as a black man. The impact of his status and identity cannot be overestimated in reaching any assessments of his judicial legacy. He was a great judge (as well as a great citizen-statesman) both because and in spite of being an African American, with all that this implied in twentieth-century United States. Few judges can lay claim to having become such a public and revered personality.

When Marshall entered the world on 2 July 1908, the United States was still a deeply racist society. Although his urban birthplace, Baltimore, was more enlightened than some other parts of the country, it still enforced a segregated system of schools, parks, and even stores; there were no restrooms for African Americans in all of downtown Baltimore. Also, in 1908, eighty-nine blacks were lynched nationally. It was not a world in which someone like the young

Marshall could expect to make much of an impression; the odds were heavily stacked against him. But it was his self-forged destiny to contribute in both symbol and substance to huge changes in tackling racism not only in the law but also in society at large.

William and Norma (Williams) Marshall were childhood sweethearts whose parents operated competing grocery stores. Both of Marshall's parents were light skinned but taught their children to be proudly aware of their black heritage. On his mother's side, his great-grandfather was a slave whose name the family never knew. He had been brought to America by slave traders from the Congo (Republic of Zaire) during the 1840s and sold to a plantation owner on Maryland's eastern shore. He was let free and, in an act of uncommon practice, married a white woman and raised his family just a few miles from his former plantation. Their son and Thurgood's grandfather, Isaiah Olive Branch Williams, became a Union soldier and then a sailor in the merchant marine. After his seafaring days, he married and settled down in Baltimore. He was an activist battler for civil rights and led the first public African American demonstration in Baltimore to protest the beatings of African Americans by the Baltimore police. On Marshall's father's side, his grandfather had joined a black regiment during the Civil War as well as the U.S. merchant regime. He eventually settled in Baltimore and married a mixed-race woman from Virginia.

As with many African Americans, William Marshall had little education and became a Pullman car waiter on the

Baltimore & Ohio Railroad's Washington-to-New York run. Blond and blue-eyed, he was caught betwixt and between and experienced a difficult life. But he made a good match with Norma, who graduated from a colored high school and went on to teachers college at Coppin State in Baltimore. She became a public school teacher in Baltimore. They both were determined to ensure that their own children would at least get a better go of things than they had. Inspired by Norma's example, William would be intolerant of poor school grades from his children.

William and Norma were married in April 1905 and had a son, Aubrey, that same year. He went on to attend the local Lincoln University. After contracting and overcoming tuberculosis, he would become an eminent chest surgeon and researcher specializing in the disease. Although he battled racism all his life, especially when struggling to locate a good hospital that would admit a black man with tuberculosis, he chose to direct his energies professionally and kept away from the political arena. This was in direct contrast to his younger brother.

Thoroughgood was three years younger than Aubrey. After spending some of his early years in Harlem, New York, the Marshalls moved back to Baltimore when Thurgood was six in 1914. At first, they moved in with his wonderfully named uncle, Fearless Mentor Williams, on Division Street, one of the better streets in old West Baltimore. Although predominantly black, this was a relatively middle-class street with not only some Jews but also Russian, German, and

Italian immigrant families. The young Marshall was named after his great-grandfather Thorney Good. But he grew tired of the long name and, in an early glimpse of his single-mindedness, shortened his name in elementary school to Thurgood, which he stuck with for the rest of his life.

Thurgood was a fortuitous combination of his parents – academically inclined, like his mother, but also a little brash and noisy, like his father. His talkative and feisty nature meant that he was always in the thick of the action and was not afraid to mix it up with the local toughs; he was street-smart as well as book-smart. At the local Division Street public school (which crammed in eight full grades), Thurgood got into his share of trouble; he was not afraid to stand up to any kids who called him any variety of racial epithets. Ironically, he would often be sent for punishment to the school basement to memorize sections of the American Constitution; he knew the Constitution by heart before he left school. This stroke of good fortune served him very well in his later life as he became one of its leading expounders.

Because the academic year for black schools was a month shorter than it was for the city's white children, Thurgood took a number of summer and part-time jobs. Graduating from his first job at seven as an errand boy for a grocery store, he began delivering hats to a hat store. On one excursion, when boarding a bus, a white man accused him of pushing in front of a white lady; he also called Marshall "a nigger." Keeping in mind his father's admonition that "anyone calls you nigger, you not only got my permission to fight him – you

Thurgood Marshall, left, around age 27 in 1935, with Donald Gaines Murray, centre. Charles Hamilton Houston is unconfirmed as the third subject of the photo. Donald Murray had been denied admission to the University of Maryland Law School, and Marshall was involved in a successful court challenge under the Fourteenth Amendment. *Source:* Library of Congress-Prints and Photographs Division [LC-DIG-ppmsca-09709]. The author wishes to thank The National Association for the Advancement of Colored People, for authorizing the use of this image.

got my orders to fight him," Thurgood came to blows with the man. Both were arrested and taken to a police station. Fortunately for his legal career (and for everyone else), no charges were laid.

In 1921, Thurgood began ninth grade at the colored Frederick Douglass school; the school had no library, no cafeteria, and no gym. Nevertheless, Thurgood thrived and graduated from high school in 1925. Thurgood had been admitted to the African American Lincoln University in Oxford, Pennsylvania – the so-called black Princeton. Even though finances were very tight in the Marshall household, his family managed to send him to college. By then, his father's drinking had become a problem. It was a strain for the family, especially for the strong-willed Thurgood, who became more and more detached from his father as the years passed and his drinking increased; he died in February 1948. Throughout that summer of 1925, Thurgood worked as a dining car waiter on the Baltimore & Ohio Railway and saved enough to begin at Lincoln.

Like many young men, Thurgood took his socializing at least as seriously as his studies. A frequent partygoer, he was a founding member of the school's Weekend Club, which bragged that they never did any schoolwork on weekends. By then, Thurgood was a tall and handsome young man who was popular among the co-eds. Indeed, he continued to attend church as much for the presence of many attractive young women as for any other reason. In his second year, he joined Alpha Phi Alpha, which was an elite fraternity of mostly light-skinned boys. However, he fell a semester behind after being injured when running to catch a ride in a pickup truck in the spring of 1928. As often occurs, this served as a wake-up call for the carousing Thurgood.

Thurgood began to focus on his studies. Impressed with the writings of W. E. B. Du Bois (who was a founding member of the National Association for the Advancement of Colored People [NAACP]) and the literature of the Harlem Renaissance, he also joined the Lincoln University debate team. Becoming one if its principal debaters, it was there that he found and developed his love for advocacy that would serve him so well in his later professional life. As importantly, he also got more serious in his romantic life. He had been dating Vivian "Buster" Burey for some time and they were married in 1929 at the First African Baptist Church in Philadelphia. With newfound responsibilities, Thurgood began to fulfill his academic potential. Graduating with honors in January 1930, he and Vivian went back to Baltimore and moved in with the Marshalls.

Although Thurgood took some premedical classes while attending college to please his mother, he determined that becoming a lawyer was to be his chosen career path. Although he had the necessary grades, attending the local University of Maryland's law school was not a viable option in the 1930s for a young African American. Thurgood never forgot this, and, years later, when the Maryland Law School named its new library after him, he refused to attend the dedication ceremony because he felt that the school was only "trying to save its conscience for excluding the Negroes." Instead, he enrolled at Howard University, which had a black student body. He was supported by Vivian and his parents; his mother pawned her wedding ring and engagement ring to help pay for tuition. For Thurgood, the stakes and the sacrifices were so high that he had no option but to do his very best. And this he did.

Thurgood was the top student in his first-year class; this won him a job as the student assistant in the law library. He was most influenced by Charles Hamilton Houston, a leading civil rights activist and lawyer, who had recently been appointed as the law school's vice-dean. The admiration was mutual, and the two struck up a professional and personal relationship. Together, they would make an institutional assault on the segregated society in which they still very much lived and worked. In 1932, while still a second-year law student, Thurgood helped Houston prepare briefs in civil rights cases. Houston told a story about both of them driving around the South from courthouse to courthouse, with Marshall in the passenger seat with a typewriter on his lap, punching out briefs as they drove. Fired up and making the best of his academic gifts, Thurgood graduated first in his class, magna cum laude.

Marshall passed the Maryland bar examination and was called to the bar on 11 October 1933. Obliged to pass on a highly prestigious Harvard University fellowship for advanced legal study because he needed to start earning an income, he opened his own practice in Baltimore, where he turned no one away and soon earned a reputation as the little man's lawyer. In 1934, he took a trip with Houston to the deep South and saw firsthand the raw world of racism at work. Even for the streetwise Thurgood, this was a gut-wrenching experience and galvanized him further in his commitment to civil rights. He did more work for the Baltimore chapter of the NAACP. His first significant victory had a sweet, ironic twist. Along with Houston, he represented Donald Murray, an African American college graduate who had been rejected by Maryland's law school solely because of his race. Arguing that such segregation by the university was "capricious and arbitrary," as no state law mandated it, they were successful in demonstrating a violation of the Constitution's Fourteenth Amendment guarantee of equality. This taught Thurgood the lifelong lesson that if "blacks were enslaved by law and segregated by law," they could still "win equality by law."

In 1936, the twenty-eight-year-old Thurgood accepted a position as NAACP's assistant special counsel. He left Baltimore and moved to Harlem, New York City, with Vivian. Despite the poor pay, they enjoyed Harlem's nightlife and after-hours jazz clubs; they partied with Cab Calloway (an old Lincoln University classmate), Alberta Hunter, and other black celebrities. Thurgood liked being a major part in an important social movement and enjoyed, at least at first, the opportunity to travel around the country, to work on the major issues of law and segregation, and to learn more directly about the ways and wiles of racism. In 1938, on Houston's retirement, Thurgood became the chief legal officer for the NAACP. Although the Treasury Department penalized its success by refusing to recognize the NAACP's tax-exempt status as an "educational" organization (resulting in the establishment of the NAACP Legal Defense and Educational Fund, Inc.), Thurgood continued and fine-tuned the policy of accepting cases that not only involved persecuted individuals but also held out the possibility of establishing a precedent "for the benefit of Negroes in general."

Thurgood Marshall's success as NAACP's counsel is now legendary. He held that position for twenty-five years and earned the fully deserved title of "Mr. Civil Rights." But his relations with other civil rights activists were not always cordial. He opposed the confrontational strategies of Martin Luther King Jr., but he was still willing to defend King and his colleagues. As for Malcolm X, Marshall disliked his belief that everything black was always right and everything white was always wrong. When they met on the street once, Marshall recalls that "I think we called each other sons of bitches and that was all there was." Nevertheless, as NAACP counsel, he won an astonishing twenty-nine out of thirty-two cases argued before the Supreme Court. This would be a stellar record for an advocate, let alone a black lawyer bringing civil rights claims in the 1940s and 1950s. His most memorable triumph was, of course, in the school desegregation case of *Brown* in 1954. He argued steadfastly and eloquently that the time had come to reverse the American tradition of racial segregation. He targeted the notorious *Plessy* case (in which the separate-but-equal doctrine was established) and sought to redeem the full emancipatory promise of the Constitution's Fourteenth Amendment. He also reported on the abuse of black soldiers in

World War II and the Korean War and, in 1959, helped draft the Kenyan constitution.

Although the *Brown* triumph of 1954 was the apogee of his lawyering career, it was also a year of personal loss. At year's end, Thurgood learned that Vivian had terminal cancer and only weeks to live. She died 11 February 1955 at the age of forty-four and after twenty-five years of marriage; they were unable to have children. He was devastated and spent the next few weeks inconsolable in their Harlem apartment. Yet, bouncing back in true Marshall style, he had remarried before the turn of the year. His new wife was Cecilia "Cissy" Suyat, a woman of Filipino ancestry who worked as a secretary at the NAACP headquarters. They had two children, who were both educated at private schools and then university. Thurgood Jr. was born in 1956, and, after a stint as a federal prosecutor, he went on to become judiciary counsel on the staff of Massachusetts's senator Edward M. Kennedy. His brother, John William, was born in 1958 and became a Virginia state police officer; he went on to be head of the U.S. Marshals Service. The running family joke was that "John locks them up, Goody defends them, and Thurgood lets them off."

In 1961, Marshall took advantage of his reputation and connections to lobby for a judicial appointment. He persuaded then attorney general Robert F. Kennedy that he warranted an appointment to the U.S. Court of Appeals. After some hesitation, Kennedy recognized the wisdom of the appointment and called in many political debts to get

Marshall nominated for the Second Circuit Appeals Court (New York, Vermont, and Connecticut). The vote on his nomination was delayed for more than eight months by Southern Democratic senators who were opposed to Marshall because of his leadership of the NAACP's Education Fund; they were placated by a deal to appoint a crony, Harold Cox, to a district judgeship in the South (which, by all accounts, was a bad appointment). On 11 September 1962, Thurgood Marshall was confirmed by a vote of fifty-four to sixteen. He was only the second African American to sit on a federal court of appeals; Marshall's friend Bill Hastie was the first.

Marshall spent a relatively quiet three years on the Court of Appeals. He contributed to 118 written opinions, of which 99 were for the majority; none of these was overturned by a higher court. He demonstrated both that he had a wider knowledge of law than his civil rights background might suggest (dealing with tort claims, admiralty cases, immigration, and patents) and that he would not rock the boat for the sake of it. In short, he kept his head down and cultivated the traditional crafts of appellate judging. In so doing, he garnered the support of many initially skeptical lawyers and politicians. But he was not universally praised. In a case of being damned if you do and damned if you don't, Marshall was criticized for being too "dull" and for "his inability to sympathize with the prosecution." For a person who had been forged in the rough-and-tumble of civil rights litigation, this was all mild fare.

On 13 July 1965, Marshall was taking his usual lunch with some fellow judges when a bailiff approached and told him that the president was on the telephone for him. "The president of what?" was his puzzled response. After a brief exchange, President Lyndon Johnson stated that "I want you to be my Solicitor General"; this position is the federal government's chief advocate. Stunned, Marshall thanked him and simply said he had "to speak with the boss, Cissy Marshall." Part of his hesitation was that this meant that he would have to give up his lifetime judicial tenure and take a salary reduction. However, he accepted the nomination and, after less than a half hour of public hearing, on 11 August 1965 the Senate confirmed Thurgood Marshall as the thirty-third U.S. solicitor general and the first African American to hold the office. The waiter's son from Baltimore had come a very long way. But he still had further to go.

As solicitor general, Marshall draped a ceremonial leopard-skin cape over his chair as a reminder of his African heritage. Being "in the dead middle of everything," he later considered this to be "maybe the best job" he ever had. Most significantly, he maintained his enviable record as an advocate; he won fourteen of the eighteen cases that he argued before the Supreme Court. Although he was able to argue some important civil liberties cases, his office obliged him to take the lead on less attractive cases; he argued that the government could imprison Muhammad Ali for refusing induction into the army, he defended the constitutionality of the war in Vietnam, and he resisted the claim that the government should have to pay for counsel for indigent suspects.

In June 1967, the conservative Tom Clark resigned from the Supreme Court and created an opening for the liberal President Johnson to fill. Not without some political risk, Johnson took the brave step of nominating Marshall – "I believe it is the right thing to do, the right time to do it, the right man and the right place." The five-day confirmation hearings were a political circus; questions ranged from the punishing to the ridiculous. Marshall was predictably assailed for his liberal approach to the Constitution and the judiciary's role. Nonetheless, on 30 August 1967, the fifty-eight-year-old Marshall was confirmed by a sixty-nine-to-eleven vote. This singular event was met with an expected division of opinion. Even some liberal sources were less than overwhelmed by his suitability; the New York Times noted that there were "far more outstanding" candidates, but "apart from symbolism, Mr. Marshall brings to the Court a wealth of practical experience as a brilliant forceful advocate." However, Chief Justice Warren was most pleased and wrote that "few men come to the Court with better experience or a sounder preparation for our work."

On 1 September 1967, Marshall privately took the judicial oath in the chambers of Justice Hugo Black, a former Ku Klux Klansman from Alabama. In a demonstration of both men's pragmatic character, they had been professional friends since Marshall and the NAACP had supported Black's nomination to the high court thirty years previously. In taking his seat on the bench, Thurgood Marshall became the ninety-sixth justice and, of course, its first African American member. The significance of this appointment and achievement cannot be underestimated in America's sordid and continuing history of social and institutional racism. In Thurgood Marshall, symbol and substance combined in powerful and compelling ways.

There is almost universal acceptance that Thurgood Marshall was a great lawyer; his record is second to none. His special skills were his sense of intuitive judgment and overall political nous; he had an acute appreciation of what causes and arguments would run best. But a separate question prompts greater controversy – was he also a great judge? As with so much about him, opinion is divided. Whereas some see him as deservedly among the front rank of judges, others view him as a more limited figure who had already done his best work at the bar but failed to attain the same level of success on the bench. The challenge then is to determine whether Marshall was able to bring together his talents and identity – legal technique, political judgment, grounded experience, combative attitude, and African American heritage – and mold them into an effective and game-changing judicial career. In becoming a judge, did he reshape himself as he conformed to what it meant to be a great judge?

Thurgood Marshall was a character of Whitmanesque proportions – "I contradict myself. I am large. I contain

Thurgood Marshall, right, special counsel to NAACP, with NAACP leaders (left to right): Henry L. Moon, Roy Wilkins, Herbert Hill. Photograph by Al Ravenna, 1956. *Source:* Library of Congress-Prints and Photographs Division [LC-USZ62-122432].

multitudes." Standing at six feet two inches tall and weighing well over two hundred pounds, he was a wonderful raconteur with a crushing handshake who tended to dominate a room. Indeed, he liked to stand out and was happy to leverage his outsider status; he wore white socks with black shoes, ordered unusual meals in restaurants for the sake of it, lived in a privileged and white enclave of Washington, and, on his appointment to the Court of Appeals, drove around in a white Cadillac with the vanity tags USJ. But he also displayed a humble side. He was beloved by those who worked for him and made time for his Episcopalian church. Even though he became a confidant of presidents and politicians and joined the Masons, he liked to keep in touch with "plain people on the street to find out how they think and feel." Although he worked hard to present himself as a simple man, Thurgood Marshall was as complex as would be expected of anyone who had made such a singular journey from a segregated school classroom to the bench of the Supreme Court of the United States.

But perhaps Marshall's largest contradiction was the one that animated his understanding of law and, therefore, his approach to judging. It was his mission and challenge to bring together his devotion to both the Rule of Law (which had played such a role in maintaining a racist society) and substantive equality; he walked that thin line between cultivating respect for existing legal rules and satisfying the need to change some rules to deliver justice. As a New Deal–Great Society supporter, he believed that racial integration could be effected through government efforts. For him, there was only a contingent, not deep, relation between racism and law. This led him to a constitutional stance that rejected any resort to legal formalism or "original intent" as being ill founded as well as conservative. Always noting that the nation's founding fathers had condoned slavery, he insisted that "the true miracle was not the birth of the Constitution, but its life, a life nurtured through two turbulent centuries of our own making." If the Rule of Law was to fulfill its vital social role, it must serve society's welfare or else perish along with it.

Inspired by such a philosophy, Marshall demanded that his fellow judges and the "knuckleheads" (his affectionate name for his law clerks, who were among the "best and brightest" students) always look to the justice of the situation and to the human experiences involved. Committed to the principle that it was the responsibility of judges to ensure that everyone had the possibility to be a full participant in a just and humane society, he saw it as his task to push the law and its judicial custodians to be ever more fair, more inclusive, and more responsive to the needs of ordinary people. He was less an activist for the disenfranchised and more a conduit through which their experiences and claims could be ensured a voice in the courts; he took seriously the idea that injustice anywhere was an affront to justice everywhere. As one commentator noted, "he knew what it felt like to be at risk as a human being" and was assiduous in impressing this on the judicial and political community. He never tired of reminding his colleagues, as in the abortion case of *Roe v. Wade* (in which he joined with Harry Blackmun's leading judgment), that law was not an abstraction but a living force in people's lives and suffering.

Having served his judicial apprenticeship on the Court of Appeals, Marshall was ready to hit the ground running on his appointment to the Supreme Court. For the first couple of years, he consolidated the liberal bloc that tended to dominate under the leadership of Chief Justice Earl Warren. However, in the spring of 1969, Warren resigned and was replaced by the Nixon-appointed and much more conservative Warren Burger. With further resignations and appointments, the court's center of gravity began to swing to the right during the 1970s. By the time that William Rehnquist became chief justice in 1986, Marshall was effectively pushed to the liberal margins. If, in the early years of his tenure, he had been "the great educator," he later became "the great dissenter." Indeed, in his last term on the court in 1990–1991, he wrote seventeen dissents, joined in on forty-one others written by his colleagues, and wrote only twelve majority opinions. Nevertheless, although often dispirited and occasionally despondent, Marshall never wavered or lost faith in his basic jurisprudential commitment to a living Rule of Law, a genuinely equal society, and justice for all. If other judges had the gift of propitious timing, Marshall did not.

It was Marshall's knack for turning the tension between the institutional pull of the Rule of Law and the substantive pull of full equality into a productive rather than debilitating force that hints at his greatness. In putting his more general values into practical operation, Marshall took a number of predictable stances: he frowned on exceptions to the Fourth Amendment's ban on unreasonable searches and seizures by government officials; he was immovable in his liberal stand that, although people were not all the same in ability or disposition, their life opportunities should not be adversely affected by the accidents of skin color, physical or mental disability, and the like; and he supported the constitutional right of women not to be deprived of an opportunity to terminate their pregnancies. As with the rest of his life, he developed the capacity to move back and forth between two very different sets of worlds and demands.

But it was his steadfastness and resolve in demanding that lawyers and judges live up to their vocational obligation to achieve justice through law that set him apart. Thurgood Marshall was one of Abraham Lincoln's "better angels of our nature" who both call others to account and themselves deliver on the deeper promise of constitutional justice. His most celebrated judgments offer a showcase of Marshall's dedication to both law and justice as one necessarily combined package. He was much more than an advocate for black America. As a compassionate man, he looked out for the interests of the underclass, both black and white. Although he did not always get it right the first time, he never ceased in his efforts to do so. This put him at odds with some of his colleagues, but he stuck to his guns and showed courage (and, if truth be told, a taste for combat) in the face of established resistance. As the sole African American on the court, this uncompromising quality cannot be ignored. He might not always have gotten his way, but he never failed to map it out or urge others to follow it.

In a series of cases, Marshall was solicitous to the pernicious effects of poverty. In *Dandridge v. Williams* in 1970, he refused to join a majority that upheld Maryland's administration of the federal Aid to Families with Dependent Children (AFDC) program that disadvantaged larger families. Insisting that the case was about more than economics, he forcefully argued that "this case, involving the literally vital interests of a powerless minority – poor families without breadwinners – is far removed from the area of business regulation" and "when a benefit, even a 'gratuitous' benefit, is necessary to sustain life, stricter constitutional standards, both procedural and substantive, are applied to the deprivation of that benefit." Indeed, he was insistent that the differential use of varying standards of constitutional review (i.e., stricter or looser standards are applied to different categories of applicants and laws) was unfair to many causes and concerns.

Again, in the 1973 case of *United States v. Kras*, Marshall reminded his less empathetic colleagues that sanctioning a $50 filing fee in bankruptcy was insensitive to the realities of how difficult life could be for the poor: "No one who has had close contact with poor people can fail to understand how close to the margin of survival many of them are – a sudden illness, for example, may destroy whatever savings they may have accumulated, and by eliminating a sense of security may destroy the incentive to save in the future." His self-imposed burden of looking out for those less able to do for themselves was the mark of his New Deal political instincts.

Marshall pushed through on this legal logic and political commitment in *San Antonio Independent School District v. Rodriguez*. Texas provided about 80 percent of the funding for all school districts, supplemented by funds apportioned by the state to local districts "under a formula designed to reflect each district's relative taxpaying ability," which meant that richer school districts generated more local school funds than did poorer districts. Although the majority held that the law had to have only a "rational basis," Marshall held firm to his view that such schemes were discriminatory and demanded the strictest scrutiny. Without mincing his words, he stated that this amounted to "a retreat from our historic commitment to equality of educational opportunity and was unsupportable acquiescence in a system which deprives children in their earliest years of the chance to reach their full potential." Succeeding in melding the Rule of Law and on-the-ground equality, it was a heartfelt plea that was backed up by a strong reliance on existing precedents that the rest of his brethren was prepared to push aside.

One of his most passionate stances was on the constitutionality of capital punishment. In a series of cases, he sustained a honed series of arguments that the death penalty was excessive, cruel, and unusual punishment under the Eighth Amendment. In perhaps the most famous and leading case of *Furman v. Georgia* in 1972, he wrote a strong dissent that captured the eloquent power and foundation of his overall jurisprudence:

> The cruel and unusual language "must draw its meaning from the evolving standards of decency that mark the progress of a maturing society." Thus, a penalty that was permissible at one time in our Nation's history is not necessarily permissible today....
>
> The burden of capital punishment falls upon the poor, the ignorant and the underprivileged members of society. It is the poor, the ignorant, and the members of minority groups who are least able to voice their complaints against capital punishment. Their impotence leaves them victims of a sanction that the wealthier, better-represented, just-as-guilty person can escape. So long as the capital sanction is used only against the forlorn, easily forgotten members of society, legislators are content to maintain the status quo, because change would draw attention to the problem and concern might develop....
>
> At a time in our history when the streets of the Nation's cities inspire fear and despair, rather than pride and hope, it is difficult to maintain objectivity and concern for our fellow citizens. But, the measure of a country's greatness is in its ability to retain compassion in time of crisis. No nation in the recorded history of man has a greater tradition of revering justice and fair treatment for all its citizens in times of turmoil, confusion and tension than ours. This is

a country which stands tallest in troubled times, a country that clings to fundamental principles, cherishes its constitutional heritage, and rejects simple solutions that compromise the values that lie at the roots of our democratic system.

Although this majestic judgment failed to sway a majority of his colleagues, it did have an effect on or, at least, contribute to a change in public opinion. Fourteen states and the District of Columbia abolished their death penalty laws, and thirty-five others revised their capital punishment statues in an effort to satisfy the procedural guidelines laid down in *Furman*. Even if Marshall's reasoning alone did not produce this response, it was a critical factor in bringing it about.

Not surprisingly, Marshall saved some of his most important contributions for the constitutional struggle over racism and the efforts to remedy its effects. In *Bakke* in 1978, the court had to determine the constitutionality of affirmative action programs in universities. After the hearings, Marshall tried to persuade his fellow justices that their leaning toward a principle of color blindness "is to make a mockery of the principle of 'equal justice under law.'" At first, there was no response, but then Harry Blackmun thanked Marshall "for his tart, biting opinion." In Justice Lewis Powell's decision for a divided court, although four justices agreed that a white applicant with superior grades had been unconstitutionally denied admission, another four (including Marshall, of course) supported Powell's view that universities *could* develop an admissions formula that took race into account. In his separate opinion, Marshall recounted in great detail the continuing shameful treatment of African Americans throughout history. He concluded that "in light of the sorry history of discrimination and its devastating impact on the lives of Negroes, . . . to fail to [bring the Negro into the mainstream of American life] is to ensure that America will forever remain a divided society." It was a ringing affirmation of all that Marshall held dear.

However, for all his energy and inspiration, Marshall had to endure a tenure on the Supreme Court in which much of the progressive momentum that he had created as NAACP counsel began to dissipate. This is no clearer than in the case of *City of Richmond, Virginia v. Croson* in his penultimate year on the Supreme Court, in 1989. With half of its population being black, Richmond made an effort to ensure that public contracts were more fairly distributed among the city's businesses by setting aside 30 percent of its local construction funds for minority business enterprises. Although a majority struck down the set-aside funds as offending the constitutional guarantee of equality, Marshall would have none of it. Joined by Justices Brennan and Blackmun, Marshall wrote with an intensity that, if anything, was strengthened by his disappointment over the court's perceived backsliding:

Today's decision marks a deliberate and giant step backward in this Court's affirmative-action jurisprudence. Cynical of one municipality's attempt to redress the effects of past racial discrimination in a particular industry, the majority launches a grapeshot attack on race-conscious remedies in general. The majority's unnecessary pronouncements will inevitably discourage or prevent government entities, particularly States and localities, from acting to rectify the scourge of past discrimination. This is the harsh reality of the majority's decision, but it is not the Constitution's command.

For the first time, a majority of this Court has adopted strict scrutiny as its standard of Equal Protection Clause review of race-conscious remedial measures. . . . This is an unwelcome development. A profound difference separates governmental actions that themselves are racist, and governmental actions that seek to remedy the effects of prior racism or to prevent neutral governmental activity from perpetuating the effects of such racism.

For some, this dissenting opinion was further evidence that Marshall had failed in his judicial mission and, therefore, subverted any claim that he was a truly great judge. In contrast with his remarkable success as an advocate before the Supreme Court, it was noted that he had not managed to convert his colleagues to his vision of constitutional justice. But this is too harsh by half. The most reasonable test of his performance is surely whether he did the best that he

Thurgood Marshall in the Oval Office, a few months before being sworn in as the first African American justice on the Supreme Court of the United States, 13 June 1967. *Source:* LBJ Library photo by Yoichi Okamoto.

could with the hand that he was dealt. And by this standard, Thurgood Marshall did that and more. He put his experience and talents in the service of an honorable undertaking and remained true to it through thick and thin. That he did so in a legal and judicial world in which he was always an outsider (and in which so many contrived to see him fail) only adds to the magnitude of his achievement. When asked how he would want to be remembered, Marshall struck the right note – "He did what he could with what he had." By that standard, he excelled himself and other contenders for judicial greatness.

Marshall had his champions as well as his detractors. There were many who considered him "an uncommon Justice" who was "a beacon to some later day when the Court might change," "a special voice that made all of us more sensitive to the legacy of discrimination," and an individual whose "vision has tipped the scales of justice in favour of a fairer and more equitable criminal justice system." But there are others who found him "more capable of advocating a cause before the bench than he was adjudicating a case while serving on it" and "less than awe-inspiring." In the controversial book by Bob Woodward and Scott Armstrong, *The Brethren*, he was notoriously portrayed (and betrayed?) as being lazy and inattentive. And even his liberal colleague, Justice William Brennan, apparently harbored doubts about Marshall's interest and commitment once he had reached the Supreme Court. None of this is surprising. Any judge who breaks the mold is bound to polarize opinion; it is almost the inevitable mark of great judging.

But it is impossible to detach any discussion about Marshall's putative greatness as a judge from the fact that he was an African American. It is as silly to suggest that race ought to be the sole criterion of judicial merit as it is to recommend that it has no importance. Race should not prevent or prioritize a contribution but rather affect its weighting and interpretation. In American society (even in the Obama years), blackness remains a significant and unmistakable marker. But, as history shows, although Thurgood Marshall is a black man, not all black men are Thurgood Marshall. The debacle over the appointment of his successor, Clarence Thomas, and his subsequent judicial career underlines this observation. A recent survey of the forty-four Supreme Court judges from 1937 to 2009 has Marshall and Thomas as the extreme bookends of the ideological spectrum; whereas Marshall made or joined the least number (21%) of conservative opinions, Thomas did so the most (82%). This gives the lie to claims about identity being all-important, but it does not reveal that it has no importance.

The impact of Thurgood Marshall on the American Supreme Court has been enormous. Although there is much more to it, his presence and self-identification as a black man was a huge part of that impact. Yet this effect was never assured; no one can be expected to carry the burden and hopes of a whole community or culture. In strictly doctrinal terms, there is nothing that he did that could not have been done by a white judge, blessed with a similar political imagination and political will. However, it was the fact that he did it that was so important. His experience as a black man meant that it was more likely (but not certain) that he would understand and champion the history and hopes of black Americans. It was more likely, because of that experience, that he would possess the political values and vision that he had. Moreover, it meant that his judgments would be more likely to be received differently (in positive and negative ways) than those of white judges. In short, the significance of his judicial career is a political story about a political figure in a political world whose signification will always be political. And a vital element of that story is that he played the judicial game, as much as he could, on his own terms, not those of others.

Consequently, to ask whether Thurgood Marshall would have been a great judge if he had not been an African American is to miss the point. He was not a great judge only because he was a black man; this is a harebrained claim. But a crucial feature of his greatness was that he did what he did when he did as a black man. It simply cannot be ignored that being an African American in twentieth-century United States carried with it a set of expectations and limitations that helped to define both white and black citizens. Although Marshall was himself able to break through and lower some of those massive obstacles to personal and social progress, he had to do so as an African American, with all that this entailed. So his standing as a great judge cannot be divorced from, even if it is not reducible to, his status as a black American. This is the beauty of Marshall's contribution; he was black, he was talented, and he made a huge difference. Like all great judges, he was a game changer.

Marshall's years on the Supreme Court were hampered by his ill health. A heavy smoker, a bad eater, and a regular drinker, he suffered from a variety of ailments – poor eyesight, shortness of breath, a weak heart, and poor circulation in his legs – that must have hampered his judicial life. But he refused to succumb. Indeed, in the late 1980s, when he was approaching his eightieth birthday, Marshall told a group of judges and lawyers who questioned him about the Supreme Court's increasingly conservative composition, "Don't worry, I am going to outlive those bastards." But his resolve and his health began to fade after the retirement of his friend and fellow liberal Justice William Brennan in June 1990. Marshall struggled on for another year but was finally persuaded to retire by the combined pressure of his wife and doctor. In his irrepressible style, on 27 June 1991 he used his last day of his twenty-four years on the Supreme Court bench to issue a withering dissent in a number of death penalty cases: "Power, not reason, is the new currency of this Court's decision making [and] the majority declares itself free to discard any principle of constitutional liberty which was recognized or affirmed over the dissenting votes." The Rule of Law was still his touchstone.

Marshall lived for only another eighteen months or so. His retirement from public life took away the main motivation that had enabled him to hold at bay the effects of his declining heath. But to the end, he lamented and gave voice to the plight of the African American. At his final press conference, he spoke about the continuance of racism in America: "All I know is that years ago, when I was a youngster, a Pullman porter told me that he had never been in any city in the United States where he had to put his hand up in front of his face to find out he was a Negro – I agree with him." He died of heart failure in Bethesda, Maryland, on 24 January 1993 at the age of eighty-four. Lying in state in the Great Hall of the Supreme Court, his body was covered with an American flag and rested on the same bier that supported Abraham Lincoln's body in 1865. This great-grandson of a slave is buried in Arlington National Cemetery.

Today, Marshall's grandfather's house on Druid Hill Avenue stands run-down and boarded-up; its Baltimore neighborhood is blighted like so many inner-city black working-class ghettos. This would no doubt sadden Thurgood. Yet it would be as great an injustice if the memory of this former resident were to endure the same fate. Posthumously awarded the Presidential Medal of Honor by President Bill Clinton in November 1993, Thurgood Marshall was many things to many people. But, most of all, he was an individual who was true to the ideals of law and justice that so animated him. He was a great man who was also a great lawyer and, I maintain, a great judge. He more than lived up to his own sense of himself. He not only "did what he could with what he had"; he did as much and more than anyone could reasonably ask of him.

The last word on Thurgood Marshall should go to some of his law clerks who wrote to him on his retirement – it captures the qualities of both the man and the judge.

Dear Judge: . . .

You have been an inspiration to all of us. Your dedication to justice, your bravery and conviction, your humor and modesty have been models we strive to emulate. It is no accident that so many of your law clerks have gone into public service – our role model was irresistible. We, too, hope "we can do what we can with what we have." We thank you with all our hearts for the improvements you have wrought in our world and for the irreversible impact you have made on our own lives. We love you, Judge.

The Knuckleheads

8

Bertha Wilson

Making the Difference

Some judges seem on a path to greatness from their early years. There often appears a direct route that leads from their early lives to their later triumphs. But there are others whose journey to greatness is more circuitous and unexpected. Their early years exhibit little that suggests that they will get the opportunity to achieve the ultimate standing that they come to occupy in society. They do not go looking for greatness. Nor is it reluctantly forced upon them. It is more the case that, simply by doing what they would normally do and being true to themselves, they stumble on greatness. Their particular talents only get a chance to be noticed and come to be appreciated when there is a propitious confluence of character and circumstance – cometh the hour and the place; cometh the woman.

Bertha Wilson is one of those judges. In the tables of great judges, she is one of those wonderful examples who confound almost all stereotypes of what it takes to be a great judge. Very much an outlier in most aspects of her life, it was only fitting that she also became one of the most feted and unique of Canadian judges. Who she was became an important dimension of what she did and, as importantly, how she was received. She did not go looking for any special place in history, but history came looking for her. And, as was the case with her American contemporaries, Sandra Day O'Connor and Ruth Bader Ginsburg, and her English successor, Brenda Hale, history found an original who made a big difference to the world of judging and those who were affected by her decisions.

Bertha Wernham was born in the old and down-at-heel seaside town of Kirkcaldy on the east coast of Scotland on 18 September 1923. Her parents, Archibald and Christina, led a modest life. As a commercial salesman in the stationery business, her father was away from home a great deal. It was left to her mother to carry much of the burden of bringing up Bertha and her two older brothers, Archie and Jim. Christina came from a simple evangelical fishing family in Fraserburgh but had trained as a nurse. Although neither she nor her husband was able to stay in school past their twelfth birthday (which was fairly standard for the time and place), Bertha's mother was fiercely ambitious for her own children. And that paid off in a big way. In addition to Bertha's own success, her brothers went on to have distinguished academic careers. Archie excelled and, after a long and successful career, became dean of the Faculty of Arts at Aberdeen, and Jim was a philosophy professor at Toronto and Carleton, Ottawa. But it was Bertha who would eclipse them.

As a very young girl, Bertha moved to Aberdeen with her family; they took in summer visitors to make ends meet. She attended St. Machar's Cathedral with her father and brother Jim. After passing the entrance exam, she went to Aberdeen Central School. Although she did well, she did not blaze any trails; she was an accomplished student rather than a brilliant one. Having always showed a gift for writing, she went on to the University of Aberdeen, where she received her undergraduate degree in liberal arts and then a master of arts. With opportunities for women still limited, she opted to obtain a teaching degree at the neighboring Aberdeen Teacher Training College. Her mother thought that would be good insurance if all else failed. But Bertha never did teach.

While a student, she met and married John Wilson. He was a student friend of her brother Jim's, and he romanced Bertha with persistence. After obtaining a postgraduate degree, he completed his studies in theology and was ordained as a minister in the Church of Scotland. A very talented student, he won the Martin Prize for Christian Evidence in his final year and used the prize money to buy Bertha's engagement ring. Even though her parents disliked John for his pacifist stance during the Second World War and rejected his left-wing political views, John and Bertha were married on 14 December 1945 in the university chapel. It was a marriage and partnership that lasted for almost sixty-two years, until her death on 28 April 2007. John only managed another year and died on 25 June 2008. If the first part of their lives centered on John's aspirations, the second was devoted to Bertha's.

John's first parish was at the Doune Church in Macduff, a traditional fishing village situated in the northeast of Scotland in Banffshire on the Moray Firth. For the first four years of their married life, Bertha fulfilled the expected role of the local vicar's wife, working in the community and supporting John in his pastoral efforts. She became leader of the local Women's Guild, the Women's Missionary Society, Girl Guides, the Youth Club, and the curling club. In these years, it was an ordinary life, but one that she fulfilled with extraordinary enthusiasm and in which she developed her passion to enhance people's daily lives, sharing in their joys and sorrows.

In August 1949, the Wilsons felt that they had achieved all they could in Macduff. Ready for a new challenge, they set sail on the *Aquitania* (in mandatory separate quarters) to Canada, where Bertha's brother Jim had already emigrated. John took up a church role in the Ottawa Valley town of Renfrew, with its rich Scottish heritage. Bertha and John established themselves as part of the community; their lives were much the same as they had been in Scotland, although there was less for Bertha to do. However, in 1952, John volunteered in the Canadian forces and accepted a post as a naval chaplain in the Korean War; he was trying to expiate his recent guilt for not serving in the Second World War. Being on her own, Bertha left Renfrew and moved to the French-Catholic working-class district of east-end Ottawa. With typical resourcefulness, she took a job as a receptionist for two dentists and savored a certain degree of independence. For the first time, her life was no longer exclusively defined as being the wife of someone.

On John's return from Korea, he was posted to the naval base in Halifax. Bertha joined him. But her appetite had been whetted, and she looked around for more challenges. Although she continued to relish her life as a vicar's wife, she determined to strike out in new directions. With John's support, she enrolled at Dalhousie University to study law. In the 1950s, law school was still very much a male preserve; there were only four other women students and two other mature students in her class. Dean Horace Read feared that "Mrs. Wilson [lacked] commitment for the rigors of the program and suggested that she would be better off taking up crocheting – law school had no room for dilettantes." Undaunted by such a crass and unprogressive stance, Bertha proved herself to be well up to the supposed rigors of law school. She put her life experience to good effect, and, when this was combined with her native intelligence, it made her a very strong student. On graduation, she received a scholarship to Harvard to complete an LL.M.

Circumstances worked against her desire to follow in the footsteps of her brothers and join academe. Once again discouraged by Dean Read, who warned her that there were no women law professors, she hesitated and decided to qualify first as a lawyer. Not surprisingly, Bertha had trouble doing so as a woman and an unconnected one at that. She ultimately found a position with F.W. Bissett Q.C., who practiced low-end divorce law and criminal work. Although it was an undistinguished beginning to her legal career, it did get her on her feet quickly and taught her the merit in representing have-not clients in a tenacious and unflagging fashion. Much like her church work, it taught her the virtues of helping those less well placed than herself. She was called to the bar of Nova Scotia in the summer of 1958.

But the Wilsons were soon on the move again. John had secured another post in Toronto; he had enjoyed the ecumenical atmosphere of the navy so much that, rather than return to a conventional ministry, he joined Wells Canada, an interdenominational fundraising organization. Bertha set about being called to the bar of Ontario and looked around for a suitable position. This time, her strong academic grades enabled her to overcome much of the Haligonian prejudice she had faced, and she was hired by the prestigious Osler, Hoskin & Harcourt law firm. Although the Toronto legal scene was not the most open of professional venues, it did provide her with the opportunity to advance her lawyering ambitions. In being the first woman hired at Osler's, she took on a role that soon became the defining motif of her legal career. In January 1968, she became the first woman to make partner at a Bay Street firm. She stayed at Osler's for a productive sixteen years in total.

While at Osler's, Bertha not only managed to accumulate a series of important firsts, but she tried to do so on her own terms. Although she was not a rock-the-boat-for-its-own-sake kind of person, she pursued her own leanings when occasion allowed. She was not entrusted with many clients of her own, but she was able to carve out an important niche for herself as a so-called lawyer's lawyer; she created an information-retrieval system that did much to revolutionize Toronto lawyers' future research habits. She flourished in the intellectual demands of her work and found that she had a particular penchant for estates and trusts work. However, she did make strenuous if unsuccessful efforts to encourage the firm to take a pioneering role in taking on pro bono work. And, in February 1968, soon after becoming a partner, she excelled herself as a traditional counsel in representing the United Church of Canada in its submissions to the Royal Commission on the Status of Women; she persuaded her client and the commission that property acquired during marriage must be viewed as the property of both the husband and the wife. In 1973, she was honored with an appointment as a queen's counsel (a not-uncommon honor bestowed on leaders of the bar).

BERTHA WILSON
Aberdeen, Scotland
*"Ego autem vivebam sine lege
aliquando."*
Always challenging the "boys" for
top spot, Bertha, (M.A. from Aberdeen University), succeeded in
copping second year honours in
Constitutional Law with the Class
of 1910 Award. Bertha claims as
her highest achievement her marriage to Parson John. And now,
'tis the Law and the Spirit! As a
student librarian Bertha had time
to read a few cases and as a result
succeeded in winning in her final
year the top Law School extra-
curricular award, the Smith Shield.
Her plans for the future are vague,
but it is rumoured that they might
include an elementary course in
plumbing!

Bertha Wilson's yearbook entry upon graduation from Dalhousie University Law School in 1957. *Source: Pharos* 1957 (Dalhousie University
Yearbook). Courtesy, Dalhousie University Archives.

In 1975, she was offered an appointment to the Court
of Appeal for Ontario, arguably Canada's leading provincial
court. Although she had acquired a wide and deep knowledge of law, she had grave doubts about the wisdom of
accepting this judicial plum; she had never argued her own
case in court, let alone judged one, and she was particularly
concerned with her lack of any criminal experience (which
made up almost 40 percent of the court's docket). Indeed, in
a response to this appellate posting (that she later described

as "the most idiotic unfeminist answers" of her entire life), she said that "I'll have to ask my husband." Nevertheless, at fifty-two, she overcame her reluctance and embarked on this next and unanticipated phase of her career. It was a decision about which she and most court watchers would remain grateful for many years to come.

Bertha was not immediately embraced by some of her judicial colleagues. Considered to be a little out of her depth, she was patronized and steered away from important or complex cases. However, by dint of her work ethic, obvious acumen, and personal manner, she won over all but the most recalcitrant of her all-male peers. Her time on the courts proved to be some of the most productive and personally rewarding years of her life. But still greater glories were in store. After a relatively short period on the Court of Appeal, she was contacted about joining the Supreme Court of Canada on the retirement of the legendary Justice Ronald Martland. The prime minister, the flamboyant and independent Pierre Trudeau, was a politician who wanted to shake up the Canadian establishment. He had already appointed Bora Laskin as the first Jewish chief justice in 1973, and he was set on making further history with a woman justice. He also knew that in appointing Bertha he would not only put a woman on the conservative court but also get someone who had definite liberal tendencies like his own. With a newly patriated Constitution and an entrenched Charter of Rights and Freedoms that same year, this was too good an opportunity to miss.

Again, Bertha hesitated. She was not in the best of health and was unsure that she was up to the rigors of such a demanding job and at such a momentous time. Moreover, she was not confident that she would be able to carry, let alone meet, the heavy weight of the expectations that were generated among women about her appointment. More immediately, it would also involve a move to Ottawa. After much soul searching and counsel from John, she agreed to make the move. John took early retirement from his church duties and assumed the role of supportive spouse in facilitating Bertha's transition to Ottawa and Supreme Court incumbency; it was a fitting payback for Bertha's own earlier devotion to his calling. She was sworn in as a judge of the Supreme Court on 30 March 1982. She was not only the first woman to sit on the Supreme Court of Canada, but also the first woman to become a member of any Commonwealth high court (but she was preceded by Sandra Day O'Connor, who became the first woman to sit on a common law country's highest court in July 1981).

But, as importantly, Bertha Wilson began a nine-year tenure that was to confirm her status as one of the great judges of Canada's or any other country's legal system. She rose to the challenge in a way that it was by no means at first certain that she would. It was not so much that she transcended her humble beginnings, her life as a vicar's wife, and the challenges of her delayed professional life. It was more that she never forgot those experiences and was able to incorporate them into her judicial outlook. For her, being a judge was one more way to help and support those in her community, even as that community grew from a small parish to a whole nation. That she did not see herself as the prototypical trailblazer might make her an odd choice as the poster-woman for legal feminists, but this was part of her appeal and what allowed her to succeed and open a path for others to follow. As the first woman judge, she intended to ensure that the Supreme Court and the legal system it topped gave due recognition to her identity and her experience.

Wilson's transition from vicar's wife to downtown lawyer to appellate judge was far from seamless. She had to battle not only her own insecurities but also the deep-grained prejudice that still manifested itself in judicial circles, albeit in a more polite and less crude manner than in earlier times. Accustomed to being a woman in a traditionally male world, she had learned to negotiate the obstacles that were thrown or fell into her path; she had often preferred compromise to confrontation. Yet she was also defiant when it came to some of her basic social commitments and long-cherished values. For her, the main challenge on joining Canada's judicial elite was to not only stand firm on her solicitude toward the disenfranchised but also to ensure that she inserted them into the style and substance of her judicial work. That she achieved so much in such a relatively short tenure is a true credit to her talents and her character.

She got a sense of the extent of her challenge, as subtle as it was strong, in her first case on the Supreme Court, *Shell Oil Company v. Commissioner of Patents*. When the judges returned to the conference room after hearing counsels' arguments, Wilson, as the most junior justice, was the last to enter the room. As she did, all the judges rose as a presumed mark of both respect and gallantry; this had never been done before. The only exception was Antonio Lamer, the next most recently appointed judge and later to be chief justice. He stayed firmly in his seat. As he much later explained on the occasion of the unveiling of Wilson's portrait at the court in December 1999, he felt that it was inappropriate to display such traditional gallantry; he preferred to "show her the greater courtesy of according her full professional respect as an equal colleague of the Court." Indeed, Wilson found the old boy's atmosphere that still persisted at the court particularly irritating. The regular process of informal consensus building that occurred either excluded her or took place in discussions around sports and other "manly" pursuits that made her feel the perennial outsider.

The more serious institutional effect of this was that she became something of a loner on the court. This had its good and bad consequences. Wilson became fiercely independent and, in a change from her earlier professional life, was less willing to simply go along with things. Unlike many of her colleagues, she did not agree that unanimous decisions carried more weight and better enhanced public confidence in the court. In contrast, she maintained that dissents and concurrences were not only inevitable but had intrinsic value because they created alternative pathways for the future development of the common law. Indeed, as she became more secure in her position, she became even more set in her principles; she refused to sign an opinion that did not reflect her view of the law, even when she fully agreed with the outcome. She participated in 551 cases that generated written reasons. She wrote for a unanimous court on 41 occasions and signed on to a unanimous opinion 213 times. However, although she wrote majority opinions twenty-two times and signed seventy-nine opinions, she wrote concurrences in more than eighty cases. Moreover, she wrote or joined more than seventy dissenting opinions. These are very high numbers and well above comparable figures for her colleagues. But she often prevailed over time when a later Supreme Court saw the wisdom in her dissent, as in the *Fidler* and *Vorvis* cases on damages for emotional distress (in which she insisted that such damages were compensatory and proper, not punitive and exceptional).

However, none of this was borne of a bloody-mindedness or vengeful nature. Although Bertha Wilson was undoubtedly stubborn in some of her views, she was determined above all else to remain true to herself, her motivating principles, and her chosen community. As a lifelong supporter (and card-carrying member) of Canada's left-leaning New Democratic Party, she insisted that judges should always be concerned with the social groups and individuals who were likely to be ignored by the political and legislative

Justice Bertha Wilson, 1988. *Source:* Rod MacIvor/Ottawa Citizen.
Reprinted by permission.

process – the poor, the oppressed, the powerless, racial
minorities, aboriginals, the young, and the criminally
accused. She was a strong proponent of the Court Challenges Program, which funded litigation on behalf of some
of these groups. In particular, she never forgot what it felt
like to be a new immigrant nor her experience, somewhat
mediated by her race and class, as "someone who lives on
the boundary between two worlds; . . . this personal duality
colours and shapes all her thoughts and actions." And, of
course, she was forever mindful of the injustices and indignities that women still had to face in Canadian society.

All this manifested itself squarely and visibly in her judgments. Wilson had little time for originalist or formalistic approaches to constitutional review. Relying very much on the Canadian concept of the Constitution as a "living tree, capable of growth and expansion within its natural limits," she considered that a principled judgment was a contextualized one. With political sensitivity and analytical rigor, she sought to "enter the skin of the litigant and make his or her experience part of [her] experience." In doing so, she wanted to make a difference in the daily lives of people; she was eager to know how a right will work "to make society better, more tolerant and more civilized." In pursuing such an approach, she exhibited and crystallized a quality of empathy that set her apart from many of her contemporaries. It was not that her judicial colleagues lacked such compassion, but that she brought it to the front and center in her professional performance.

Yet she was never cavalier in her approach to existing precedents. Often impatient with the idea that the past must temper present responses to new social situations, she worked hard to square her judgments with extant legal doctrine where possible. Indeed, her work ethic was second to none. It infuriated her that her fellow judges failed to work with what she saw as professional efficiency and allowed a substantial backlog to develop – "Is there any solution to this problem or is it just something the first woman on the Supreme Court is expected to endure?" And she expected the same degree of efficiency and effort from her own clerks.

Two of her most dynamic contributions came as a judge on the Ontario Court of Appeal. *Pettkus v. Becker* in 1978 addressed the case of Rosa Becker, who ran a beekeeping farm for more than fourteen years with her common law partner, Lothar Pettkus. They shared expenses and labor, but the farm was solely in the name of Lothar. When they broke up, Rosa sought a one-half interest in the farm. Wilson wrote a unanimous and pathbreaking judgment for the court. She held that the support and labor provided by the female partner created a constructive trust by which Lothar held the farm and other assets for the joint benefit of both of them. She insisted that any other outcome would continue to unjustly enrich men at the expense of women. Her decision was upheld by the Supreme Court of Canada, which adopted her approach as a convincing crystallization of an important shift in communal and common law values.

In the case of *Bhadauria v. Seneca College* in 1979, it had to be decided whether there existed a common law tort of discrimination that the highly qualified Mrs. Bhadauria could avail herself of in her rebuffed efforts to become a teacher. In a bravura judgment of understated persuasion, Wilson found that, although no authority had previously recognized a tort of discrimination, none had actually repudiated the existence of one. Drawing on both precedent and policy, she fashioned a judgment that built a tort from the ground up. In particular, she held that the existence of a human rights code did not preclude the development of such a right but actually strengthened the case for one: "If we accept that 'every person is free and equal in dignity and rights without regard to race, creed, colour, sex, marital status, nationality, ancestry, or place of origin,' as we do, then it is appropriate that these rights receive full protection of the common law." As the Supreme Court said, this approach was "a bold one and may be commended"; modern judges were not at all disposed to develop new torts or causes of action. However, the court felt that the code had entirely occupied the field and stymied the further development of the common law. Wilson's judgments in *Bhadauria* and *Pettkus* set in motion trends that were to run throughout her career on the Supreme Court – an adherence to strong principles of fundamental justice, an unwillingness to compromise on them, and an unwavering compassion for the outsider.

Wilson's tenure on the Supreme Court coincided almost exactly with the first decade of the Charter of Rights; this constitutional "bill of rights" was introduced in April 1982 and brought the courts more into the political spotlight. As a democrat, she might have crafted a different scheme of protecting people's basic entitlements. But, as a judge confronted by the enormous task of evaluating government action against the Charter's guarantees, she deferred to the current state of affairs and tried to work out the new relationship between legislatures, executive, and the courts in the most productive way she could. As she often replied to critics of judicial activism, "we didn't volunteer" for Charter duties. Her self-imposed task was to work these changes to the advantage of the more deprived members of Canadian society. Accordingly, she was much less willing to defer to Parliament than many others. In applying the Charter's section 1 reasonable limits test, she set the evidentiary bar very high for government to justify its presumptive incursions on people's liberty. Her body of judicial opinions stands as a fitting monument to her sincerity, her mission, and her greatness.

Although her judgments on the Supreme Court cover a vast range of issues, she was consistently a champion for the underdog. A particularly telling judgment of hers was *Singh* in 1985. A Sikh refugee claimed that he was entitled to an oral hearing and to know the case to be met before being deported. Wilson delivered an uncompromising judgment in support of the claim. Holding that the recent adoption of the Charter "sent a clear message to the courts that the restrictive attitude which at times characterized [the courts'] approach to the *Canadian Bill of Rights* (a federal piece of legislation) ought to be re-examined," she decided that "everyone" in section 7 includes every human being physically present in Canada. Further, she held that the protection of a person's "life, liberty and security" and his or her entitlement to "fundamental justice" needed to be interpreted broadly. The fact that this would vastly increase administrative costs was beside the point. Although her judgment was devoid of rhetorical flourish, she set down a marker that other judges would have to respect in future cases.

Wilson continued this line of reasoning in later Charter cases. In the *Edmonton Journal* case in 1989, which was about the validity of publication bans, she again wrote a concurring judgment that supported the decision that such bans infringed on the Charter's section 2 guarantee of "freedom of expression." Abandoning any trace of an originalist or abstract approach to constitutional interpretation, she insisted that a contextual approach was the preferable approach to Charter claims: "[This approach] recognizes that a particular right or freedom may have a different value depending on the context. [As such,] the contextual approach attempts to bring into sharp relief the aspect of the right or freedom which is truly at stake in the case as well as the relevant aspects of any values in competition with it." Although a quite technical and legalist issue, its resolution by Wilson offered further evidence of her insistence that the Charter should be understood and activated in the real world of ordinary Canadians' lives.

In a similar vein, in *Guerin*, Wilson stood onside with Canada's aboriginal peoples. An Indian band had surrendered valuable surplus reserve lands to the Crown for lease. Wilson wrote concurring reasons (for Ritchie, McIntyre, and herself) that went beyond the majority and held that there existed a special type of fiduciary duty that the Crown owed to native individuals and groups; the government was obliged to act only in the best interests of aboriginal people.

Again, short on stylistic flair but long on principle, Wilson came through on her commitments with professional kudos and personal integrity.

Most assuredly, Wilson drew a line in the sand when it came to the protection of women. The *Lavallee* case in 1990 dealt with an abused woman who had killed her abuser; the specific issue in the case centered on whether a psychiatrist could give expert evidence on the mental state of "battered wives." Writing for the majority of the court, she acknowledged that the ordinary man standard that is traditionally applied to self-defense was inapplicable in such circumstances because "men do not typically find themselves in that situation: . . . the definition of what is reasonable must be adapted to circumstances which are, by and large, foreign to the world inhabited by the hypothetical 'reasonable man.'" On this basis, she held that, unless the psychiatrist's evidence – that Lavallee's shooting of her abusive husband was "a final desperate act by a woman who believed she would be killed that night" – was admissible, the jury would be left with little more than unreliable popular mythology about domestic violence and the women who endure it. In genderizing the law (or, at least, allowing for gender-sensitive rules), she was fully living up to the expectations that she and others had placed on her.

Was Wilson a great judge simply because she was a woman or, at least, the first woman on a nation's highest court?

This question looms large over her career and contribution. The answer is as complex as the assumptions on which the question is based. There can be no doubt that her identity as a woman played a significant role in her own sense of what a judge should do, and it showed in many of her judgments. However, as with Thurgood Marshall (see Chapter 7), one would be sadly mistaken to reduce her quality as a judge to her identity alone; this would involve falling into the same trap as those who maintain that identity has no role in understanding the judicial performance of men and women. Although Wilson's experience and identity as a woman cannot be ignored in any assessment of her judicial performance, nor can it be the only criterion by which to categorize her as a great judge. She was never not a woman and yet never only a woman.

In 1990, Bertha Wilson published a lecture in which she sought to answer a pressing question for her and others – will women judges really make a difference? Surveying a considerable amount of legal literature, she came to the opinion that "a distinctly male perspective is clearly discernible" in many areas of law, especially criminal law, which is "based on presuppositions about the nature of women . . . that are little short of ludicrous." In order to combat this bias, she endorsed institutional efforts to reeducate and sensitize male judges to these problems. However, she insisted that it would be necessary to appoint increasing numbers of women judges if any genuine or substantial progress were to be made. Wilson argued that the

Bertha Wilson, left, with two Chief Justices, Antonio Lamer and Beverly McLachlin. *Source:* Courtesy of Jeannie Thomas.

appointment of women judges not only will provide important role models for women and alter the dynamics of courtroom demeanor, but also could "establish judicial neutrality through a countervailing female perspective." Wilson suggested that women judges will bring a different experience to the task and responsibility of judging:

> The universalistic doctrine of human rights must include a realistic concept of masculine and feminine humanity regarded as a whole, that human kind *is* dual and must be represented in dual form if the trap of an asexual abstraction in which *human being* is always defined in the masculine is to be avoided. If women lawyers and judges through their differing perspectives on life can bring a new

humanity to bear on the decision-making process, perhaps they *will* make a difference. Perhaps they will succeed in infusing the law with an understanding of what it means to be fully human.

This essay, published in the midst of her judicial career, provoked a huge debate. Some were very critical of her importation of a feminist perspective into the law; they maintained that courts were no place to pursue ideological agendas. Others took her to task for her failure to advance sufficiently a feminist approach to law and justice. There is some force to each of these observations. If she was a feminist, it was one of a very liberal variety. She saw the individual as a fundamental building block of society and had concerns about injustices to any individual, woman or man. She maintained that the best way to overcome the obstacles faced by women was to favor liberal strategies that were available to all people. In this way, she sought to construct a vision of justice that cut across traditional categories of identity and embraced all victims of oppression and injustice. But the challenge and fate of women were never far from her thoughts and remained a priority.

Wilson's impassioned and confident belief in the transformative power of women judges (and, by implication, judges who are from traditionally excluded or disadvantaged minorities) is not to be taken lightly. It is a conceit of established groups (white, male, heterosexual, etc.) to maintain that a cold objectivity is the only touchstone of true knowledge. But she was overreaching if she intended to claim that women will have a necessary and consistent impact on the law and craft of judging simply by virtue of being women. Biography surely counts, but not in any predetermined or formulaic way. The appointment of women judges will increase the likelihood that women's different social experiences will be brought to bear on judicial decision making. Context will influence and be influenced by such participation; there are no global or essentialist truths that people possess by virtue of their black, female, or gay lives. It is not the *will* in "perhaps they will make a difference" that should be stressed, but the *perhaps*.

In some circumstances and locations, identity alone may speak louder than any words of explanation or indignation. As Wilson insisted, the influence that more women and black judges can have as role models in law and society generally should not be underestimated. As shown by the careers of Bertha Wilson herself and her later female colleagues on the Supreme Court of Canada and other similar institutions, there is nothing that these women have done as judges that could not have been done by their male counterparts, and there is nothing that is consistently "feminist" among them. But the importance of the fact that they have done them as women judges cannot be gainsaid. This is true for many decisions by Wilson, especially *Lavallee* and *Pettkus*. Yet, she did not always take the woman's side. In *Pelech*, she declined to reopen a fifteen-year-old maintenance order against a husband, even though the wife had fallen on very straitened circumstances; she reasoned that an individual's rights sometimes had to be preserved at the cost of gender-based equality.

But her distinctive voice is best remembered for her concurring judgment in *Morgentaler*. In concurring in the majority decision to strike down the criminal limits on the availability of abortion, she brought a distinctly "female" approach to the issue of abortion:

> The question then becomes whether the decision of a woman to terminate her pregnancy falls within this class of protected decisions. I have no doubt that it does. This decision is one that will have profound psychological, economic and social consequences for the pregnant woman. The circumstances giving rise to it can be complex and varied and there may be, and usually are, powerful considerations militating in opposite directions. It is a decision that deeply reflects the way the woman thinks about herself and her relationship to others and to society at large. . . .

> It is probably impossible for a man to respond, even imaginatively, to such a dilemma not just because it is outside the realm of his personal experience (although this is, of course, the case) but because he can relate to it only by objectifying it, thereby eliminating the subjective elements of the female psyche which are at the heart of the dilemma. Women's needs and aspirations are only now being translated into protected rights.

In this judgment, Wilson blended together her own past experiences as well as her professional disposition. While in Ottawa in the early 1950s and working as a dental receptionist, she had been asked to counsel and console a patient who sought an abortion. The pregnancy turned out to be a false alarm, but Bertha never forgot the psychological turmoil this woman went through in trying to decide what to do. Although never a mother herself and not instinctively supportive of abortion in general, she found herself "totally unable to condemn the woman for the choice she would have made." This compassion, earned through her earlier experience, was incorporated into a series of technical arguments that produced a signature judgment. At the basis of her judgment was the individualistic belief that "liberty in a free and democratic society does not require the state to approve such decisions, but it does require the state to respect them."

Of course, the Supreme Court's *Morgentaler* decision provoked strong reaction. Wilson seemed to bear the brunt of people's feelings. She received a flood of letters following the decision; some criticizing her, some thanking her, and some offering to pray for her. After her retirement, she received a letter from Henry Morgentaler himself. In it, he told her that

> I found your judgment . . . inspiring and uplifting. While the other judges in the majority ruling decided the matter on narrow procedural grounds you, and only you, were upholding articulately human dignity, female self-esteem,

freedom of religion and fundamental freedoms in a truly democratic society. It was a breath of fresh air and a judgment that will forever remain a milestone in Canadian history.

The good doctor seems to have hit the nail on the head.

Bertha Wilson retired from the Supreme Court on 4 January 1991. Still well short of the mandatory retirement age, some would say that she left far too early. But, in a letter to Justice Minister Kim Campbell, she acknowledged that her energy was ebbing, that the workload was rising, and that she "should move over for those at the height of their powers." Some would say that she never fully realized her potential and that, as such, she fell short of the greatness that she might otherwise have claimed. This assessment is unduly harsh. Although a longer tenure on the court might well have further burnished her reputation, I maintain that she had done enough by breaking the mold and creating an important space for others to work to be counted among the ranks of great judges. She may not be able to boast of a weight of precedents or a canon of leading judgments that measure up to the contribution of generations of earlier, male Canadian judges, but her relatively short time on the bench left as deep and telling a mark as any of them. She was a genuine and acknowledged pathbreaker and deserves full credit for that.

Nevertheless, despite her flagging health, she still managed to maintain a hectic pace of public life. In 1991, not only did she agree to chair the Canadian Bar Association's Task Force on Gender Equality in the Legal Profession, but she also became a commissioner for the Royal Commission on Aboriginal Peoples, which lasted for five years. In both these roles, she remained true to her convictions and contributed to influential reports on both fronts. She died at the age of eighty-four after a long illness on 28 April 2007. She had by then been honored with nineteen honorary degrees. She had packed more into her short professional career, and to a greater effect, than almost anyone else.

She proved that being a good judge is not about identifying and following one way of doing things; there were lots of ways that the judicial task could be performed that were different from the traditional and male-dominated ways of old. For her, though, it was not enough for a judge to go her own way. A great judge was one who was able to persuade others, by argument or example, of the merit of their approach and open up a space for those that followed to pursue their own particular muse. And this is exactly what Bertha did. Other women judges on the Supreme Court, like Claire L'Heureux-Dubé, Beverly McLachlin, and especially Rosalie Abella, have honored her example not necessarily by aping her views and values but by trying to be the best judges that they can be and in the way that they think that they should be. Throughout her life, she remained true to her modest roots, even as she grew and became, against her instincts, an icon for many.

At the end of the day, Bertha Wilson showed that you could take the girl out of Kirkcaldy, but you could not take Kirkcaldy out of the woman. In 1989, Beverly McLachlin was appointed to the Supreme Court of Canada. Along with Wilson and Claire L'Heureux-Dubé, she became the third woman to sit on the court. At her swearing in and as the judges lined up to take the traditional group photograph, Bertha Wilson leaned over to the new judge and said in her unmistakable Scottish brogue, "Three down, six to go!" The girl from Kirkcaldy had come a long way and, as sure as scotch eggs are eggs, made all the difference.

9

Albie Sachs

Of Struggles and Lies

The best way to understand how and why people do what they do is not always to rely on their own explanations. Although such accounts cannot be ignored entirely, there is little reason to place exclusive weight on them, especially if they are retrospective. People often do things for very different reasons than they think. And, on occasion, they act for reasons that are quite the opposite of what they think. Not surprisingly, this is equally true of judges. In striving to understand how and why judges judge as they do, their own explanations are simply one source of elucidation. While it is essential to factor in these personal introspections, it is also important to treat them with a healthy degree of skepticism. Of course, the more reflective and self-critical these reflections are, the better and more reliable they might be.

Some judges, like Tom Denning (see Chapter 6), seem to lack any genuine capacity for serious self-scrutiny; they draw on their deeper instincts and insights with few qualms or equivocations. Others, however, possess a rare ability to step back and give their initial arguments and conclusions a rigorous cross-examination. One of those who has possessed such a quality and sought to incorporate it into his judgments is the singular Albie Sachs. A South African whose life was as far from that of the traditional judge as any likely could be, he managed to negotiate that informative dynamic between the demands of judicial office and the hard-earned experience of his personal life with a rare and revealing aplomb. A full appreciation of his legal judgments and his autobiographical musings offers a portrait of a complex man who wrestles with as he embodies what it means to be great judge.

Albie Sachs lived a life that follows closely the historical arc of his nation's own life. Born as a relatively privileged person into the racist horrors of South Africa, devoting himself to the long struggle to bring about a more just world, and making a standout contribution to a new polity, his career highlights the impact that a committed and courageous individual can have on the rest of the world. As much as anything else, his life and career redefine what it means to be a lawyer and a judge in a society that is grappling with the injustices of its past and the ameliorating opportunities of its future. Still alive, Albie Sachs is a one-of-a-kind judge.

Albert Louis Sachs was born in Johannesburg on 30 January 1935. His parents, Emil Solomon Sachs and Ray Ginsberg, had been young Lithuanian Jewish immigrants. Whereas his father, Solly, was an uncompromising leader of the Garments Workers Union who was loved and loathed in equal measure by his members and the racist government, his mother was a typist for Moses Kotane, the South African Communist Party's secretary general. The defining thread of their lives was more to create a classless society than to achieve a Zionist state. The marriage lasted a decade, and, as a young boy, Albie moved to Cape Town with his mother and his younger brother. He had little sustained contact with his father. But, on his sixth birthday, in the middle of World War II, he received a card from his father that had a lasting impact – his father expressed his hope that Albie would grow up to be "a proud soldier in the fight for liberation." As such, his nature and nurture prepared him to be an active player, not only a passive spectator, in South Africa's history.

A fairly precocious child, Albie went to the South African College School. When he was thirteen, apartheid was officially introduced in South Africa under Prime Minister Daniel François Malan; this formalized the raw divisions between the races that were already sordid facts of Albie's life. He gained early admission to the law faculty at the University of Cape Town. At the young age of seventeen, in his second year, he cut his activist teeth by taking part in the Defiance of Unjust Laws Campaign. In 1952, he and three other young people were arrested for sitting in an area of the General Post Office that was reserved for nonwhites. These actions of civil disobedience set Albie on an emancipatory path that he would pursue for the rest of his life and that would give direction to most of his judicial decisions.

In June 1955, Albie attended the ANC-dominated Congress of the People at Kliptown in the black township of Soweto, near Johannesburg; this led to the adoption of the Freedom Charter, which became the inspirational manifesto of apartheid's opponents. He completed his legal studies and was called to the bar at the beginning of 1957, shortly before his twenty-second birthday. Putting the Freedom Charter principles into effect in his professional and personal life, he turned his legal practice over to the defense of blacks, minorities, and antiapartheid activists. At this time, he fulfilled the awkward role of being a lawyer in a patently unjust legal process. Not surprisingly, he became suspicious of law as anything other than an oppressive force in people's lives and did as much to challenge the Rule of Law as to uphold it; he gave daily substance to the idea of the lawyer as a civil disobedient.

By the early 1960s, the challenge to apartheid was becoming more insistent and more violent. The government introduced even harsher laws and gave even greater discretion to the security forces. Having developed closer ties to the ANC leadership and become increasingly more active in his lawyering, Sachs was arrested in 1963. He was initially kept in solitary confinement for ninety days under

Albie Sachs as a young advocate. *Source:*
Courtesy of Albie Sachs.

the despised ninety-day law, by which prisoners could be
kept in detention without any court appearance, any charges
being laid, or any explanation offered as to why they were
being detained. Sachs refused to cooperate with his cap-
tors and was held for the full ninety days. However, on
his release, he was immediately rearrested at the detention facility's gates and brought back into custody. He was
held for another seventy-eight days before he was finally

released. Once he left the facility that time, he ran until he reached the ocean and threw himself in out of sheer relief.

After that incident, Albie was a marked man. For the next two years, he was prohibited from "gathering" with more than one other human being at any given time and from publishing anything. Needless to say, his legal practice ground to a halt. He was arrested again in 1966; the police sought information about one of his friends, Fred Carneson, who had been charged with sabotage. Although his detention was for a shorter period, he was subjected to more brutal treatment. Tortured through sleep deprivation, he considered this to be the most terrifying incident in his whole life and "a moral defeat, it was basically humiliating." He calls it "the worst, worst moment of my life." In David Edgar's dramatization of Sachs's book, *The Jail Diary of Albie Sachs*, Albie recalls that, as bad as his treatment was, it did not compare to that of the black prisoners – "I was locked up, while blacks and coloureds were being sleep-deprived. And I was sleep deprived, while blacks were beaten up. And whites are being beaten up, and non-whites getting tortured with electric shocks."

Dispirited and depleted, Sachs left South Africa for England within a couple of months of his second detention. The government granted him permission to leave "on condition that he never return." He reconnected with his secret girlfriend, Stephanie Kemp, who was a former client in South Africa and had been charged with some explosives-related offenses; they married in 1966. He took up graduate studies in law and earned his doctorate at Sussex University in 1970. During this time, he also published his first book, *The Jail Diary*, and completed his second book, *Stephanie on Trial*, which is about his experiences defending her activist efforts. Albie took a teaching position at the University of Southampton and immersed himself in his scholarly work. His thesis was published as *Justice in South Africa*, and later he coauthored *Sexism and the Law*. He stayed in contact with the ANC and campaigned actively as part of the antiapartheid movement. A stateless refugee for a considerable amount of time, he was automatically excluded as a "terrorist" from visiting the United States. In 1977, he moved to the newly independent Mozambique. He and Stephanie were divorced soon afterward; their sons, Alan and Michael, remained with her in London.

Sachs was excited by the prospects for reform and progress in Mozambique following the revolution against colonial Portuguese rule in 1975. He soon became fluent in Portuguese and became a professor of law at Eduardo Mondlane University in the capital, Maputo. Along with other ANC exiles in Mozambique and neighboring Tanzania, Albie cemented a close relationship with Oliver Tambo, who was by then the ANC president-in-exile. Between 1983 and 1988, he became director of research in the justice ministry in Mozambique. Around this time, he also became a member of the ANC Constitutional Committee and was asked to write a code of conduct for ANC fighters, especially dealing with the treatment of captured members of the South African

Forces. Sachs was adamant that the ANC must not stoop to the methods of the hated security forces. His drafted code of conduct placed strict anti-torture regulations on the ANC and was subsequently implemented. In a comment made at the end of his judicial career, Albie confessed that "of all the legal writings I have done in my life, two stand out as being far more important than any of my books or judgments: the one is a tiny note I smuggled out of jail after I had been tortured by sleep deprivation, and the other is [the] Code of Conduct."

In 1988, one of the truly decisive experiences of Sachs's remaining life occurred – an assassination attempt. Early on the morning of 7 April, Sachs was planning to drive to the beach to go for a run. When he opened the driver's side car door, a bomb exploded. Fortunately, although his car was totaled and he was thrown a considerable distance, he survived. He was taken to a nearby hospital by passersby. So dazed was Sachs that he thought he was being kidnapped by his rescuers. He ultimately lost most of his right arm and the sight in one eye. Although there were clear indications that the South African government was responsible for the bombing (and Sachs later met with the security officer who helped to plan the attempt, Henri van der Westhuizen, as part of the Truth and Reconciliation process), no person was ever prosecuted or held directly accountable. Albie entered a lengthy period of convalescence during which, as testament to his dogged determination, he learned, among many other things, to write with his left hand. In 1989, he also became director of the South African Constitution Study Centre at the Institute of Commonwealth Studies in London.

The impact, both physical and psychological, of this event on Sachs cannot be underestimated. Rather than shy from publicity or hide his mangled body, Sachs sought out publicity as a way of creating a galvanizing spectacle out of his injuries and recovery – "This is my vengeance, my way of fighting back, not by killing others, but by transmuting bad into good, using my heart and brains to project as much as possible a vision of survival, struggle, triumph and humanity." He was never shy about putting his stump to strategic work when it suited him. And he became passionate about having things of beauty around him. He developed a habit of only wearing bold and bright (some might say garish) shirts. Indeed, the tall and lanky Sachs, with his unfilled shirtsleeve often waving like a personal flag, cut an unmistakable figure in the more traditional venues of the courts. As one commentator rather harshly noted, he personified "the vivid aspect of a mercurial Picasso clown, with mottled red and white skin and off-center blue eyes." He wore his battle scars with pride.

As far as Sachs was concerned, the attempt on his life merely redoubled his commitment to the struggle against apartheid and to creating a more just society. Following Nelson Mandela's release in February 1990 and the imminent collapse of the apartheid regime, Sachs returned to South Africa and began to play an important role in the shift to constitutional democracy. He was appointed as an

ANC representative in the negotiations for a new constitution for South Africa and pushed for an expansive bill of rights. But, in 1994, Sachs was appointed directly to the new, eleven-member Constitutional Court of South Africa by the then President Mandela. Before entering the judiciary, he felt obliged to step aside from party politics and give up his membership in the ANC. Taking up judicial office was the quintessential put-your-money-where-your-mouth-is moment for Sachs. After years fighting against an oppressive legal system, he finally had the opportunity and, as importantly, the responsibility to put his ideas into action. As a judicial debutante, his success at meeting this challenge would be the measure not only of his own mettle but also of his claim to greatness as a judge.

The Constitutional Court began its first sessions in February 1995. Sachs played a leading role in the design and construction of a new courthouse on the site of a former high-security prison on the Braamfontein ridge in Johannesburg; he is justly proud of the building and its symbolic openness. All eleven judges usually hear every case unless there are conflicts or other reasons for recusal. Unlike other supreme courts, the court's function is to determine the meaning of the Constitution in matters that come before it. The court also had a special role in the process of drafting a new and final constitution for South Africa. Sitting as the Constitutional Assembly, Parliament produced a constitutional text, and then the court had to certify that all thirty-four Constitutional Principles agreed on in advance by the negotiators (of whom Sachs was one) of the Interim Constitution had been respected. With Sachs's involvement and approval, the court initially found that this was not the case. The new text had to be revised before it became the law of the land.

If there was one theme that characterized Sachs's approach to public office, it was that of 'soft vengeance.' Many might be forgiven for adopting a stance of retributive or hostile reprisal. Instead, Albie decided that he would exact revenge against his political opponents by refusing to subject them to the kind of deprivations and disrespect that they imposed on him and his fellow activists. He followed the Gandhi-inspired Desmond Tutu, archbishop and Nobel Prize winner, in believing that you best "destroy the enemy by making him into a friend." He is also fond of quoting Harold Washington, first black mayor of Chicago – "No matter where you are, you cannot escape my fairness."

From the get-go, Sachs was clear eyed about the enormity of the task facing him. As a lawyer, he had been a rebellious part of a corrupt and oppressive legal process that turned the Rule of Law and its attendant virtues into a pervasive evil. Although there was much that was new about South Africa, legal tradition was a potent force among the older and still influential members of the legal community. As Sachs acknowledged, "the legal community is by its nature both conservative in thinking, yet restless for change." Hence the dilemma facing judges of deciding whether to locate themselves as the upholders or the reformers of established legal principle. Sachs seemed to sense that the most prudent and practical course would be to play both sides against the middle – a difficult and dangerous enterprise. He decided that he would not get very far by projecting and implementing a radical or entirely personalized view of the Constitution. Instead, he ran the risk of being labeled a milquetoast or even a sellout by some former colleagues and fellow travelers. He developed a judicial philosophy that used as its baseline the criterion that any judgment must strike the legal community as reasonable, or "defensible, if not totally convincing." Preferring pragmatic progress to ideological purity, he planted his judicial flag in this inviting, if perilous, territory.

Sachs put this into operation by formulating and hewing to what he calls the three Cs of good judging in a constitutional democracy – civility, courage, and collegiality. He gave each of these a particular and typically idiosyncratic bite. For him, civility was not merely politeness or "good manners" but extended to "respecting people who differ from yourself... [and] maintaining a framework within which you can debate and discuss." He cultivated an appropriately gracious, if no-nonsense, atmosphere in his dealings with colleagues, counsel, and litigants. Being courageous meant having that elusive quality of steadfastness and a determination to say and do what is right; this approach might not always be conducive to harmony, but, if expressed civilly, it fosters mutual respect. As for collegiality, he insisted that this was an "absolutely fundamental quality of a good judge." Although it meant that he had to learn to hold his tongue on occasion, he believed that collegiality and occasionally solidarity were important lessons from his younger ANC days. He saw this not as a compromise of conscience but rather as a better and more effective way to advance a shared agenda of social justice. Of course, there are times when it is not possible to be both courageous and collegial, but that situation was to be handled with civility at least.

Indeed, Sachs seems to have done some of his most important work behind closed doors. By general standards, he was far from a prolific judgment writer. Nevertheless, by the norms of the Constitutional Court, he wrote more than the average number of judgments. He did not write a single leading judgment during his first two years on the court, but he did write eight separate concurring opinions. His first leading, but co-written, judgment was in 1997; he authored his first solo leading judgment only in 1998. As he found his judicial feet (mindful that, unlike many of his colleagues, he had never held judicial office before), he began to write more confidently and carried more than his equal share on the court. Although he was not afraid to dissent (and, when he did, he tended to write rather than only vote), he made a habit of writing separate concurring judgments; he wrote many more concurring judgments than his colleagues.

However, although Sachs maintained confidences and never tittle-tattled on his colleagues, it is apparent that he devoted considerable effort to working the halls and offices of the Constitutional Court; he was instrumental in the frequent workshopping of judgments and the ensuing exchanges around them. In its first eleven years, the court had a roughly 80 percent unanimity rate; this included not only decisions with no dissents but also those with no separate concurring opinions. Sachs did much to bring this about and refers to the Constitutional Court as "possibly the most collegial court in the world; . . . we want everything that comes out of the court to be rigorous and good and respected." This collegial practice gave a gifted operative and practiced politician like Sachs an extended, if unheralded, opportunity to influence his colleagues and the law in important ways.

In *Mhlungu*, one of its earliest cases, the Constitutional Court of South Africa had to determine at what point the new constitutional protections kicked in. Section 241(8) of the Constitution stated "all proceedings which immediately before the commencement of this Constitution [27 April 1994] were pending before any court of law shall be dealt with as if this Constitution had not been passed." In an important criminal case around confessions and the death penalty, the accused were allegedly involved in a murder in April 1993. An indictment in Afrikaans was served on them on 11 March 1994 and re-served in English on 4 May 1994; the trial commenced on 18 May 1994. If the proceedings were considered pending on 27 April, the accused would not be entitled to any potential benefits under the Constitution; if they were not, they would. Several thousand other

Albie Sachs, right, speaks to the ANC Kabwe Conference in Kabwe, Zambia, 1985. The ANC passed Sachs' proposed code of conduct, which he developed at the behest and with the support of ANC president-in-exile Oliver Tambo. The Conference was under the protection of the Zambian military, fearing an assault by South African commandos. Also pictured in the foreground are, l to r: John Nkadimeng, Oliver Tambo, and Thomas Nkobi. *Source:* Courtesy of Albie Sachs.

prosecutions (and, therefore, likely acquittals) depended on the outcome of the *Mhlungu* case.

By a majority of seven to four, the court held that the proceedings were not pending and that the accused should receive the benefits of any relevant constitutional rights. All the judges agreed that it was imperative that the court approach its constitutional responsibility with a liberal sense of the larger political context and that a purposive approach to such interpretive matters was required. Nevertheless, as Justice Kentridge for the minority put it, "there are limits to the principle that a Constitution should be construed generously . . . and those limits are to be found in the language of the Constitution itself." He held that judges must resist the temptation to engage in "divination" rather than interpretation. In response, Justice Mahomed's opinion for the majority insisted that substantive justice must trump legalistic interpretation; he treated section 241(8) as being only about preserving the continuing authority of pre-Constitution courts.

In a judgment of genuine subtlety and analytical power, Sachs set out his own methodological stall. Forming part of the majority, he took a line of reasoning that challenged the interpretive frameworks of both Kentridge and Mahomed. Whereas he criticized Kentridge for giving "far too little weight to the overall design and purpose of the Constitution," he maintained that Mahomed unnecessarily stripped section 241(8) "of its more obvious meaning." Insisting that there was a "need to distinguish between grammatical exegesis and constitutional analysis," Sachs maintained that "the issue is how to reconcile the two sets of provisions when they collide with each other, not how to interpret each on its own." In balancing the technical provisions of the "puny" section 241(8) against the "powerful" provisions that entrenched fundamental freedoms, he chose to read back the former in light of the latter. Throughout his judgment, Sachs was at pains to stress that his judgment "is not a case of making the Constitution mean what we like, but of making it mean what the framers wanted it to mean; we gather their intention not from our subjective wishes, but from looking at the document as a whole." By way of conclusion, Sachs revealed his broader jurisprudential stance:

> I might add that I regard the question of interpretation to be one to which there can never be an absolute and definitive answer and that, in particular, the search of where to locate ourselves on the literal/purposive continuum or how to balance out competing provisions, will always take the form of a principled judicial dialogue, in the first place between members of this court, then between our court and other courts, the legal profession, law schools, Parliament, and, indirectly, with the public at large. . . . The objective of my approach is to preserve the essential functional core of section 241(8), while causing the minimum disturbance to the fundamental rights entrenched in Chapter 3. In other words, instead of mechanically applying section 241(8) and then lamenting, ignoring or minimizing the injustices which follow, the court gives effect to the gravamen of the section, but construes it in such a way as best to harmonize with [the fundamental freedoms] and so avoid needless incongruity and eliminate unnecessary postponement of enjoyment of fundamental rights.

This was a judgment by which Sachs claimed for himself a stance as someone who could be praised by his former revolutionary comrades and by his current judicial colleagues. Managing to move seamlessly between high theory and down-to-earth practice, he demonstrated that law and politics were not separate universes, but, in the right hands, could and must be mutually reinforcing discourses. *Mhlungu* stands as a wonderful prototype of top-level judging at its best. He came to the "progressive" decision but held fast to a principled approach to constitutional adjudication.

For Sachs, as he says, "every judgment I write is a lie," in that the polished presentation of judicial pronouncements tends to disguise the cobbled-together and protracted thought processes and drafting that go into every judgment. He maintains that, because there never is one singular or objectively right answer to any legal dispute, the judge can never be on "rational autopilot" – "Although the elements to be put into the scales are objectively defined, the weight given to each individually, and the overall balance to be achieved when all are put together, could vary from arbiter to arbiter." In this sense, Sachs frames the judicial task as being about both choice and constraint as well as freedom and responsibility. It is his willingness not to hide that fact, to struggle in its shadow, and to do so with a refreshing candor that places him in the vanguard of great judges.

When evaluating any career, there is a difficult choice to be made. One way to proceed is to look at the overall sweep of a person's work and try to assess its collective and cumulative merit; this means toting up the more prosaic performances with the pathbreaking ones. The other is to concentrate on the standout occasions and to downplay the rest; this necessitates a certain occlusion of vision. In Sachs's case, the former is probably a fairer route to follow, as it is his effort to sustain a particular attitude to judging that is his forte; his success was as much about how he arrived at his decisions as about what he did. Although most of his decisions are hardly unpredictable if you know something about the man, it is his crafted and principled stance as well as his genuine effort to square his ingrained values with established legal norms that catches one's attention. However, a sense of that honorable approach can be gleaned from some of the leading cases in which he delivered important judgments.

His commitment to soft vengeance was put to the test in two cases involving alleged mercenaries. In *Basson*, a doctor was charged with not only supplying the drugs used to kill antiapartheid political prisoners but also administering them himself. The problem was that these acts had taken place in other countries. In a public commentary on his judgment, Sachs asked, "[d]o we bend the law, because of the horror of what he has done? If we do that, what were we fighting for? We were fighting *for* the rule of law, *for* constitutionalism." In an open and candid reflection, he describes finding that an appeal application should be heard according to the law as he understood it, but "the sheer gravity of the crimes . . . is not a reason for relaxing the legal principles at stake" when they are applied to those who are "the enemies incarnate of the rule of law."

In a second case, South African mercenaries were intercepted while traveling to Equatorial Guinea to carry out a violent coup. Ironically, the mercenaries' families sought the protection of South African law for the out-of-country fighters. Sachs maintained that, although the Constitution could not be enforced against another country, the South African foreign affairs office was nonetheless under an obligation to try to ensure that the South African mercenaries were treated fully in accord with international law and not subjected to torture.

In *Lawrence*, one question was whether or not the prohibition of the sale of liquor on a Sunday contravened the Constitution's guarantee of religious freedom; the applicant shopkeepers were not religiously driven in their challenge and merely sought to use the constitutional provision for their own commercial benefit. Sachs was clear that, even if partly secular in intent, the statute was built on a Christian base. Emphasizing that the statute reflects an attitude of "favouritism coupled with indifference, rather than one of orthodoxy combined with persecution," Sachs upheld the statute, as any economic or religious disadvantage created by the Sunday liquor restriction is relatively minor in comparison with the goal of reducing alcohol consumption. Throughout his judgment, he was concerned with the "symbolic effect" of the law on non-Christians (like himself). In reaching his decision, he applied what he calls the "reasonable South African" standard, an individual "(of any faith or of none) who is neither hyper-sensitive nor overly insensitive

Perhaps more than that of any other judge, Sachs's judicial career presents the challenge of how judges are to traverse that crucial ground between personal political commitments and public judicial expectation in the starkest terms. Sachs is a man of touted and battle-forged values; there is a lifetime of writings and speeches about his personal credo on politics or life. However, as a lawyer, he understood that a judge cannot always or easily collapse personal commitment into judicial pronouncement. As a judge, he was obliged to accept that he represented not only himself but also a movement and a nation. For good and bad, he saw himself as the custodian of a very special privilege – to build a nation that was true not only to itself and its past but also to the best ideals of constitutional democracy. It was a public undertaking that had to incorporate, but not be eclipsed entirely by, a private vision of politics and the good life.

For most of Sachs's legal career, the government and process were the problem. He came to understand law and justice as being not merely disconnected but actually in relation to each other; apartheid was a constitutional deviation from it. So, when he came to sit on the bench of a new nonracial South Africa, he had to make a readjustment in his basic outlook by integrating law and justice. The challenge was that he would overcompensate and see the ANC-dominated government as the final word on what was right and just. Acutely aware of this risk, he sought to fashion a role that suited the unique conditions in which he was required to exercise his judicial

to the belief in question, but highly attuned to the requirements of the Constitution." This is a very diplomatic and delicately balanced judgment that displays Sachs's intellect and sensitivity to fine effect; he managed to effect a synthesis that does justice to his theoretical concerns and his practical values.

Again, in light of South Africa's and Sachs's own past, the issue of whether a prisoner should be able to vote in elections loomed controversial. In *August v. Electoral Commission*, this matter was given a particular twist, as it involved whether correctional institutions have an obligation to help facilitate the registration and voting of prisoners. In interpreting the constitutional right to vote, Sachs rejected entirely the government's argument that, because "prisoners are the authors of their own misfortune," the state cannot be expected to foot the infrastructural and financial bill for helping them vote. Dispensing with a series of technical arguments advanced, he went so far as to say that merely granting prisoners a right to vote will be an empty entitlement if they are not permitted to have resources spent on them to actualize that crucial democratic right: "Rights may not be limited without justification and legislation dealing with the franchise must be interpreted in favour of enfranchisement rather than disenfranchisement." Although the issue at hand was not of seismic proportions (and its resolution not unexpected considering Sachs's own past), he offered a very strong argument about why it might be considered essential to treat rights as acting as swords as much as shields against disabling government policies.

Perhaps the case that best brings together Sachs's commitment to substantive political justice and his desire to craft compelling legal arguments is *Fourie*. This case was about the validity and availability of same-sex marriage. After a Denning-esque opening, Sachs's judgment confronted this highly controversial issue with a delicate but firm conviction. The legal impediment to their marriage was the use of "husband" and "wife" in the governing Marriage Act and their common law definition. Speaking for a nearly unanimous court, Sachs decided that the legal exclusion of same-sex couples from the institution of marriage contravened their constitutional equality rights. Again, emphasizing the importance of giving rights a positive spin, he insisted that

> [the Constitution] cannot be read as merely protecting same-sex couples from punishment or stigmatisation. [It] also go[es] beyond simply preserving a private space in which gay and lesbian couples may live together without interference from the state. Indeed, what the applicants in this matter seek is not the right to be left alone, but the right to be acknowledged as equals and to be embraced with dignity by the law. Their love that was once forced to be clandestine, may now dare openly to speak its name. The world in which they live and in which the Constitution functions, has evolved from repudiating expressions of their desire to accepting the reality of their presence,

and the integrity, in its own terms, of their intimate life. Accordingly, taking account of the decisions of this Court, and bearing in mind the symbolic and practical impact that exclusion from marriage has on same-sex couples, there can only be one answer to the question as to whether or not suc' couples are denied equal protection and subjected to ur discrimination. Clearly, they are, and in no small de

Although the court stopped short of declaring gious bodies be required to perform same-sex m observed that "it would be wrong and unhel opposition to homosexuality on religious ç an expression of bigotry to be equate gave the government one year to ch modate same-sex marriage. Outs closed minds, Sachs's argumer common ground and bring to a compliment to his assu ceeded in reconciliatior ously. It was his shar came to the fore. conscious motiv "experience i shapes yo' the way betwf its

prow

to the belief in question, but highly attuned to the requirements of the Constitution." This is a very diplomatic and delicately balanced judgment that displays Sachs's intellect and sensitivity to fine effect; he managed to effect a synthesis that does justice to his theoretical concerns and his practical values.

Again, in light of South Africa's and Sachs's own past, the issue of whether a prisoner should be able to vote in elections loomed controversial. In *August v. Electoral Commission*, this matter was given a particular twist, as it involved whether correctional institutions have an obligation to help facilitate the registration and voting of prisoners. In interpreting the constitutional right to vote, Sachs rejected entirely the government's argument that, because "prisoners are the authors of their own misfortune," the state cannot be expected to foot the infrastructural and financial bill for helping them vote. Dispensing with a series of technical arguments advanced, he went so far as to say that merely granting prisoners a right to vote will be an empty entitlement if they are not permitted to have resources spent on them to actualize that crucial democratic right: "Rights may not be limited without justification and legislation dealing with the franchise must be interpreted in favour of enfranchisement rather than disenfranchisement." Although the issue at hand was not of seismic proportions (and its resolution not unexpected considering Sachs's own past), he offered a very strong argument about why it might be considered essential to treat rights as acting as swords as much as shields against disabling government policies.

Perhaps the case that best brings together Sachs's commitment to substantive political justice and his desire to craft compelling legal arguments is *Fourie*. This case was about the validity and availability of same-sex marriage. After a Denning-esque opening, Sachs's judgment confronted this highly controversial issue with a delicate but firm conviction. The legal impediment to their marriage was the use of "husband" and "wife" in the governing Marriage Act and their common law definition. Speaking for a nearly unanimous court, Sachs decided that the legal exclusion of same-sex couples from the institution of marriage contravened their constitutional equality rights. Again, emphasizing the importance of giving rights a positive spin, he insisted that

> [the Constitution] cannot be read as merely protecting same-sex couples from punishment or stigmatisation. [It] also go[es] beyond simply preserving a private space in which gay and lesbian couples may live together without interference from the state. Indeed, what the applicants in this matter seek is not the right to be left alone, but the right to be acknowledged as equals and to be embraced with dignity by the law. Their love that was once forced to be clandestine, may now dare openly to speak its name. The world in which they live and in which the Constitution functions, has evolved from repudiating expressions of their desire to accepting the reality of their presence,

and the integrity, in its own terms, of their intimate life. Accordingly, taking account of the decisions of this Court, and bearing in mind the symbolic and practical impact that exclusion from marriage has on same-sex couples, there can only be one answer to the question as to whether or not such couples are denied equal protection and subjected to unfair discrimination. Clearly, they are, and in no small degree.

Although the court stopped short of declaring that religious bodies be required to perform same-sex marriages and observed that "it would be wrong and unhelpful to dismiss opposition to homosexuality on religious grounds simply as an expression of bigotry to be equated to racism," Sachs gave the government one year to change the law to accommodate same-sex marriage. Outside persons with entirely closed minds, Sachs's arguments managed to establish a common ground and bring together divergent groups. It was a compliment to his assurance and his style that he succeeded in reconciliation where none seemed to exist previously. It was his shared experience of being an outsider that came to the fore. At the time, this did not appear to be a conscious motivation on his part. As he later reminisced, "experience is experience – it becomes part of your being, it shapes your responses and your reactions, your intuitions, the way you tend to lean one way or the other when choosing between different forms of persuasive reasoning, each with its own internal rationality, that lead to different outcomes." As such, his *Fourie* judgment is a fitting monument to his prowess as a judge and his reputation as a great judge.

Perhaps more than that of any other judge, Sachs's judicial career presents the challenge of how judges are to traverse that crucial ground between personal political commitments and public judicial expectation in the starkest terms. Sachs is a man of touted and battle-forged values; there is a lifetime of writings and speeches about his personal credo on politics or life. However, as a lawyer, he understood that a judge cannot always or easily collapse personal commitment into judicial pronouncement. As a judge, he was obliged to accept that he represented not only himself but also a movement and a nation. For good and bad, he saw himself as the custodian of a very special privilege – to build a nation that was true not only to itself and its past but also to the best ideals of constitutional democracy. It was a public undertaking that had to incorporate, but not be eclipsed entirely by, his private vision of politics and the good life.

For most of Sachs's legal career, the government and legal process were the problem. He came to understand law and justice as being not merely disconnected but actually in opposition to each other; apartheid was a constitutional norm, not a deviation from it. So, when he came to sit on the bench in the new nonracial South Africa, he had to make a massive adjustment in his basic outlook by integrating law with justice. The challenge was that he would overcompensate by treating the ANC-dominated government as the final arbiter of what was right and just. Acutely aware of this risk, Sachs struggled to fashion a role that suited the unique conditions under which he was required to exercise his judicial

Justice Albie Sachs with three law clerks, c. 2000. Clerks, clockwise from left: Farzana Badat, Deepak Gupta and Zanele Majola. *Source: Courtesy of Albie Sachs.*

authority. He did this by avoiding a doctrinaire or dogmatic approach. Instead, although he respected the commitments of the government to social justice, he was often prepared to intervene where necessary and strike down legislation. It was not so much that he abandoned a political approach to judging but that he massaged and amended the nature of those politics so as to better meet the particular demands of the judicial undertaking. For Sachs, therefore, the adjudicative function was politically distinctive and distinctly political.

This pragmatic perspective was not to everyone's liking. Some complained that Sachs had often been too quick to assume that the government (which he helped bring to power) had the best of intentions when, in fact, this might have been far from the case. In the area of access to health resources, Sachs was seen as too willing to drag his feet and defer to the government's claims about the scarcity of available resources; he went along, albeit reluctantly, with his judicial colleagues in some cases in easing the pressure on the government. Indeed, this particular issue points out the general predicament in which he found himself. In his early days, he was in the trenches with many who went on to assume government office, so he was sensitive to their plight and loyal to their values. However, as a judge entrusted with implementing constitutional guarantees, he had to distance himself from those former friends and stand in judgment of them. More than most, Sachs managed to achieve a workable balance, but it is not surprising that he occasionally tripped up and found himself in the uncomfortable position between a pragmatist's rock and an idealist's hard place.

Some critics concentrated on Sachs's love of art and culture and drew attention to what they thought was an incongruous "bourgeois" side to this self-proclaimed revolutionary. Claiming that he made too much of a transformation in his personal shift from freedom fighter to judge, they alleged that he became an unlikely apologist for the kind of depoliticized legal outlook that he had agitated against for so long. Sachs's initial response to this was that art and culture are themselves instruments of struggle. In the same way that culture can transcend local politics, so law can connect to values that are "deeper" and "more profound" than any particular struggle. Of course, this retort did not placate all critics. A few treated this as more fuel for their critical fire, as they saw Sachs drawn toward an overly Westernized vision of law and rights that neglected the need to nurture and reflect a truly African jurisprudence. But Sachs was unrepentant and, although he relented on the revolutionary role of art and culture, he remained unmoved in his view that "political pluralism, representative democracy, the rule of law and the notion of good government . . . have the potential to undermine existing power relations and to open up the way to substantial social, economic and political advance by the majority [who are not currently in power]."

However, Sachs did seem to get ahead of himself when he treated soft vengeance as a magnanimous gesture. If the main thrust of the notion of soft vengeance is that even one's worst enemies should be granted the legal entitlements that were denied to Sachs and other freedom fighters, then it seems wrongheaded. Being protected against torture and other indignities ought to be available as of right, not as indulgence from a condescending victor. The Rule of Law and its accompanying rights are available to people simply because they are human, not because of the vengeance, soft or otherwise, of the new state. It is unsettling when former revolutionaries come close to crowing about their moral superiority when all they are doing is what they expected and demanded of their own oppressors. Although Sachs succumbed to such temptations only on occasion, it smacks of an unnecessary triumphalism.

Another relatively blind spot for Sachs, like for so many strong judges, was that he was not as sensitive as he might have been to the issue of the disputed legitimacy of judges' enormous power to discipline democratically elected lawmakers, especially in the constitutional context – who is to judge the judges? Sachs seemed unconcerned by this specter and was content to insist that "we don't exercise power, we restrain power." Indeed, he saw a larger and more pressing problem to be the need to ensure the further independence and the integrity of the Constitutional Court and its judges; the interference of the executive branch of government must be assiduously resisted if the judges are to fulfill their constitutional mandate. Sachs thought that it required both the government and the judiciary to live up to their institutional ideal if justice were to be achieved. In this, he observed that a delicate balance is required when actually claiming and asserting that independence: "You don't want to be striking down everything the government does just to show that you are independent."

Albie Sachs retired from the Constitutional Court in 2009, after fifteen years of judicial service. He now lives in a small beach bungalow in Cape Town (near to the original home where he lived with his mother) with his new partner,

Vanessa September, and their young son, Oliver. He still wears his flamboyant shirts, writes regularly, and is an enthusiastic cheerleader for the Constitutional Court and its crucial job in South African society. His 2009 book, *The Strange Alchemy of Life and Law*, is a literary tour de force that offers an autobiographical glimpse at the enigmatic individual who is Albie Sachs; it is an entertaining account that captures the modest and narcissistic as well as the defiant and defensive about him. Yet his important legacy comprises the deeds that he accomplished, the struggles in which he fought, the judgments that he rendered, and the fluency that he attained in both legal and political languages. He is a rare character among judicial ranks and one who turned the potential disadvantage of political involvement into one of exemplary success.

Unlike many others, becoming a judge was not part of his life plan. Indeed, the odds of doing so in his native South Africa were remote at best when he entered law school in 1950. However, when he did, no one was more surprised or pleased than him – "And so it came to pass that if some people are born to be judges and some achieve judicial office, I was one of those that had judicial office happily thrust upon him." He fulfilled that role as best he could and, in the process, made a special contribution not only to his country's progress but also to the world's view of what it means to be a judge in transitional societies. In a self-effacing assessment of his own career, he paid tribute to those comrades-in-struggle who achieved so much, and he tried

to characterize his own efforts as a judge as "trying my best
in a particular context at a particular moment to deal hon-
estly and openly with the issues before me – I try to make
my voice as legally clear, true and harmonious as possible."
It is a credit and example to all lawyers and all judges everywhere that he undertook such an effort and realized it more
often than not.

10

Judging the Future

A Leap in the Dark

There are few generalizations that can be made about what it takes to be a great judge. If the previous eight chapters have any unifying thread, it is that there is no proven or assured way to become or be recognized as a great judge. And perhaps that is what best defines greatness. It is the willingness of some judges to be different and make their own mark that sets them apart from their colleagues. Great judges recognize that there is no playbook that can be consistently relied on to get the job done. It is a mark of some judges' greatness that, consciously or otherwise, they are prepared to do it their way – they rewrite in whole or part the playbook itself. These people are originals who, by example and excellence, reveal a way of being a judge that makes what has gone before no longer quite so obvious, acceptable, or ennobling.

The test of good judging might well be less about getting it right than about doing it well. But the test of great judging is about not only doing it well but doing it in a way that obliges others to rethink what is involved in judging well. Great judges are more accepting of law's rule-based existence and less naïve about politics' promise of transformation. In short, they recognize that they are situated within an official tradition of legal reasoning but insist that there is ample room to experiment within and, as importantly, with its confines. They play as much with the rules of the game as within them. Because they treat adjudication as a ludic exercise of the most serious dimensions, such judges are not stymied or troubled by law's apparent fixity or brute thereness. Whereas others experience limits and restrictions, they see openings to be explored and opportunities to be grasped. For them, the primary task of adjudication is about imaginative creativity as much as anything else. In great judges' hands, law is something to be reworked into a better and more fulfilling image of itself. Although good judges are lauded for their technical abilities in parsing cases and rooting out inconsistencies, great judges are celebrated for their vision and inventiveness.

Of course, there are grave dangers with such an approach to the fulfillment of judicial duties. There is a thin line between a great judge and a merely idiosyncratic or rogue judge. In marching to the beat of their own drummer, judges can often go off in unappealing or unhelpful directions. Instead of leading their colleagues down new and fruitful paths, they wander away into a relative wilderness where no one else is minded to follow. This ability to persuade others, directly or indirectly, to follow is a neglected dimension of what it takes to be a great judge. It may not occur in a judge's lifetime, but it must occur. By luck or good judgment, the beat of a judge's own judicial drummer must resonate with others and pull his or her more traditional peers along. A great judge may begin as a band of one but must usually recruit some companions to his or her innovative cause.

There is also the considerable challenge of how to square the great judge's performances with a political system that considers government to be best when it is for and *by* the people. In a perfect or more ideal democracy, it is surely the case that, insofar as there are judges who resemble the current incumbents, the best ones might be those who are prepared to glow dimly rather than shine brightly. Citizens – not their judicial consuls, no matter how gifted or progressive – should rule themselves. But, in societies in which the judicial role is considered to be a vital and legitimate part of a constitutional democracy, it will not be judges who hide behind fictions about following and applying rules, rather than creating and transforming them, who will fulfill their parts best or most appropriately. Great judging demands an essential degree of candor and integrity. And this must include the acknowledgment that there is no way to follow the rules that does not involve a creative and political dimension. Great judges are those who grasp that truth

and commit themselves to working within as they transform existing traditions of adjudication and constitutional
politics. As Herman Melville said of literary geniuses, great
judges "are parts of the times; they themselves are the times,
and possess a correspondent coloring." They put the color in
the times, and, in so doing, they light up their societies in
ways that others never glimpsed or imagined.

Of course, as the media coverage of court decisions
becomes more extensive and bruising, it would not be an
auspicious prospect for all judges to do what great judges
do. Any system can handle only so much creativity and often
only in occasional bursts: if my proposed set of great judges
were to sit together in a Supreme Court for the ages, they
would not be a "dream bench." Indeed, a great judge can only
be great because most of his or her colleagues are not; greatness suggests a break from the pack, no matter how talented
or praiseworthy most judges are. But, without such disrup-
tive and unsettling interventions, the law will atrophy and
fail to fulfill its daunting potential. It is the burden and
blessing of great judges that they do what other judges do
not, cannot, or will not do. In the spirit of Alexander Pope,
such judges know that "if to repeat is good, to transform is
great." They understand that, to achieve the rewards of success, it is vital to run the risks of failure. Playing it safe is
simply not in their attitude or almanac.

Praising any particular judge as great is not at all to
suggest that he or she has hit on the perfect or purest way
to judge. The fact that there is a batch of great judges and

that they differ widely among themselves in their approach and attitude is ample evidence of that. Nevertheless, the eight judges profiled in this book seem to accept that, like so much else, judging is what you make it. And, because it has been made, it can be remade in different and competing ways. There is no one tried-and-true program for greatness. These rarest of performers do not think of themselves as allotted actors in another's story. Instead, they take law's narrative and the judicial craft in directions and to places that other, lesser lawyers did not glimpse or imagine. Such singular and uncommon individuals reinforce the idea that the best among us are not those who can perfect an action but those who, reinventing what it is that we do, can advance a new way of thinking about and doing what is important. Great judges are distinct trendsetters (even if reluctantly or unintentionally so), not dedicated followers of prevailing fashion.

Looking back over the careers of these one-of-a-kind judges, it soon becomes obvious that there are no guidelines for identifying the most propitious confluence of circumstances and character that is likely to give rise to a great judge. Although there are some similarities among some of the judges, they are more than balanced out by the differences among them. Indeed, the collective biography of these great judges recommends against any temptation to single out or prioritize any one particular set of conditions or traits.

Keeping in mind that judicial greatness is the complex and serendipitous interaction of personal character and historical circumstance, how these factors interact and coalesce will be as unique as the individuals themselves. Some of these factors include:

- *Background* – There is no one particular background that can guarantee success. Although it no doubt helps to be born into circumstances of privilege rather than deprivation, the octet of judges surveyed in this text came from varied backgrounds. Some were born to privilege (William Murray and Oliver Wendell Holmes Jr.), but others dragged themselves up from humble roots (Thurgood Marshall, Bertha Wilson, Albie Sachs, and James Atkin). And still others were somewhere in between (John Marshall and Tom Denning). Of course, to become and remain judges, they must to some extent have bought into the prevailing structures of power and authority wherever they started out.
- *Ideology* – There is no discernible pattern to the values and prejudices that particular judges had to hold to be counted among the ranks of great judges. Again, it is important that a possible candidate for greatness does not possess views that fall entirely outside the mainstream of popular opinion but instead works the seams. However, great judges have traversed a wide spectrum of political and social views; there is no party line. Some judges took a stance that largely endeared them to

established interests (William Murray and Oliver Wendell Holmes Jr.), but others were prepared to buck the trend and challenge the status quo (Bertha Wilson and Thurgood Marshall). Also, some saw their roles as decidedly political (Thurgood Marshall and Albie Sachs), whereas others did not (James Atkin and William Murray).

- *Timing* – There can be no doubt that, like comedians, judges must possess the gift of good timing if they are to have any chance of breaking into the select group of great judges. But, whereas some judges clearly benefited from being in the right place at the right time (John Marshall and Bertha Wilson), others were part of the creative forces that made the timing right for change (Thurgood Marshall and Albie Sachs). It is not enough to be at a point in history when change is possible. It takes a special something to turn that opening to actual transformative effect. Great judges make their own timing.

- *Longevity* – It seems likely that a long career offers the best chance for assuming a leadership role, but it is insufficient by itself. Although some judges enjoyed a long tenure on the bench (Tom Denning and John Marshall) and others had a much shorter stay (Bertha Wilson and Albie Sachs), this alone did not mark them as great or not. A judge's performance in certain crucial cases might be a better indicator of his or her greatness (James Atkin and Oliver Wendell Holmes Jr.) than his or her overall performance across his or her career. General consistency is not always to be preferred to selective excellence in assessments of greatness.

- *Popularity* – It is important not to confuse greatness with popularity. Any judge who breaks the mold is bound to polarize opinion; this is almost the inevitable mark of great judging. Even though some judges remained popular (John Marshall and James Atkin), others (Oliver Wendell Holmes Jr., Tom Denning, and Thurgood Marshall) generated as much controversy as approval over their careers. But they still garnered almost universal support for their recognition as great judges; they were great judges both because of *and* despite their foibles and flaws. Doing good, whichever way it is assessed, is not a requirement for being a great judge.

- *Character* – Although some great judges were larger-than-life characters, others were not. Leadership was something that they demonstrated both by loudly standing out and by quietly setting an example. Some courted the limelight (Oliver Wendell Holmes Jr., Tom Denning, and Albie Sachs), some could not avoid it (Thurgood Marshall and Bertha Wilson), and others hid from it (James Atkin). There is no one personality type that matches up with what it takes to be a great judge, and there is no ideal character who is bound to become a great judge.

- *Style* – It clearly helps as a judge to have a distinctive style of writing; literary or rhetorical flourish adds a mark of quality to a judge's work. However, the great judges identified in this book ranged from the memorable (Oliver Wendell Holmes Jr. and Tom Denning) to the forgettable (John Marshall and Bertha Wilson) in terms of their writing style. What seems to matter more is whether they found and articulated a distinctive voice that resounded through their judgments and through their own society. Great judges have found their own voice and captured the listener's ear.

Taken together, these observations confirm that greatness can come in many shapes and sizes; there is no one-size-fits-all guide to greatness. What it takes to become and be acknowledged as a great judge defies simple elucidation or formulation. However, while common law systems require most judges to follow rather than lead, the vibrancy of the common law allows and occasionally expects a judge to branch out and experiment with new modes of judging. Some become great judges not only because of what they do (and they usually achieve plenty), but also because of the pioneering example that they set for others of what might be done. My great judges met as they reset the conventional standards for what it means to be a good judge. Indeed, those heralded judges give the lie to the traditional claim that a judge's role is to stay out of the limelight in the political wings. Whereas good judges must know their place, great judges make their own place. And, in the process, they clear a space for others to create their own places.

If history is any guide, it seems clear that Chief Justice John Roberts's formula for judging – "Judges don't make the rules; they apply them" – is unlikely to propel him or others who take a similar view into the select group of leading judges. This seems the guiding creed of the middling judge, not the great one. In contrast, it is in the quality of greatness to lead, not to follow. In the same way that Mozart, Shakespeare, Ellison, and Dickinson did not become the great artists that they were by aping others and hewing to the customary rules of their chosen craft, so great judges do not become recognized as such for their capacity, no matter how refined and exemplary, to do what others do. They have the courage of their own convictions in not only coming to the decisions that they do, but also doing so in a way that best achieves what they take to be the most compelling performance of the judicial task. They transform the law by also changing social understandings about what is involved in being that law's judges.

When Thurgood Marshall said that he hoped that he would be remembered most for the fact that "he did what he could with what he had," he was being a shade disingenuous. If his own career is anything to go by, he knew that the measure of greatness was that you did much more than could reasonably be expected with what you had. And, like his fellow great judges, this is what he did. Great judges not only outdo their colleagues, but they excel themselves in so doing. The legal world is changed by their efforts and is fated, for both better and worse, never to be the same again.

Marshall and the other individuals in this book were game changers. Unafraid to take a leap in the dark, they were prepared like others to "act for the best, hope for the best and take what comes." But, unlike most others, their leaps into the future have often brought law and judging to a more illuminating representation of itself.

References

Chapter 1. In Search of Great Judges: Playing by Their Own Rules

Secondary Sources: Books and Articles

Abraham, Henry J. *The Judiciary: The Supreme Court in the Governmental Process*, 10th ed. (New York: New York University Press, 1996)

Burke, Edmund. "Preface to the Address of M. Brissot to his Constituents" in *The Works of the Right Honourable Edmund Burke*, new ed., vol. 7 (London, UK: C & J Rivington, 1826–27).

Gunther, Gerald. *Learned Hand: The Man and the Judge* (New York: Knopf, 1994).

Holmes, Oliver Wendell, Jr. *Collected Legal Papers*, ed. by Harold Joseph Laski (New York: Peter Smith, 1952).

Holmes, Oliver Wendell, Jr. *The Common Law* (Cambridge, MA: Belknap Press of Harvard University Press, 2009).

Hutchinson, Allan C. *Is Eating People Wrong?: Great Legal Cases and How They Shaped the World* (New York: Cambridge University Press, 2011).

References

Hutchinson, Allan C. *It's All in the Game: A Nonfoundationalist Account of Law and Adjudication* (Durham, NC: Duke University Press, 2000).

Keeton, Robert E. *Venturing to Do Justice: Reforming Private Law* (Cambridge, MA: Harvard University Press, 1969).

Llewellyn, Karl. "The Adventures of Rollo" (1952) 2 U. Chi. L. Sch. Rec. 3.

Nietzsche, Friedrich Wilhelm. "Ecce Homo," trans. by Clifton P. Fadiman in *The Philosophy of Nietzsche* (New York: Modern Library, 1954).

Pederson, William D. & Norman W. Provizer, eds. *Great Justices of the U.S. Supreme Court: Ratings and Case Studies* (New York: Peter Lang, 1994).

Posner, Richard A. *How Judges Think* (Cambridge, MA: Harvard University Press, 2008).

White, G. Edward. *The American Judicial Tradition: Profiles of Leading American Judges*, 3rd ed. (New York: Oxford University Press, 2006).

Secondary Sources: Websites

Cook, E. M. *"Latin for the Judgin'*: A critical edition" *Ralph the Sacred River* (28 July 2005), Blogger, http://ralphriver.blogspot.com/2005/07/latin-for-judgin-critical-edition.html.

Cases

Brown v Allen, 344 US 443 (1953).

Candler v Crane, Christmas & Co., [1951] 2 KB 164 (CA).

Chapter 2. Lord Mansfield: A Long Journey

Secondary Sources: Books and Articles

Campbell, J. *The Lives of the Chief Justices of England*, 3 vols. (London: John Murray, 1849–1857).

Denning, the Rt. Hon. Lord. *What Next in the Law* (London: Butterworths, 1982).

Denning of Whitchurch, the Rt. Hon. Lord. *From Precedent to Precedent* (Oxford: Clarendon Press, 1959).

Fifoot, C. H. S. *Lord Mansfield* (Oxford: Clarendon Press, 1936).

Heward, Edmund. *Lord Mansfield* (Chichester, UK: Barry Rose, 1979).

Holdsworth, W. S. "Blackstone's Treatment of Equity" (1930) 43 Harv L Rev 1.

Holliday, John D. *The Life of William Late Earl of Mansfield* (London: Elmsly and Bream, 1797).

Hulsebosch, Daniel J. "Nothing but Liberty: *Somerset's Case* and the British Empire" (2006) 24 LHR 647.

Kayman, Martin A. "The Reader and the Jury: Legal Fictions and the Making of Commercial Law in Eighteenth-Century England" (1997) 9 Eighteenth-Century Fiction 373.

Morris, G. L. "Lord Mansfield: As He Then Was" (1954) 12 U of Tor Sch of L Rev 29.

Mullett, Charles. "Lord Mansfield and the English Dissenters" (1937) 2 Mo L Rev 46.

Murphy, Bridget. "*Luke v Lyde*: Lord Mansfield and the Development of the Principles of Mercantile Law" (2000) 9 Auckland UL Rev 1140.

Oldham, James. *English Common Law in the Age of Mansfield* (Chapel Hill: University of North Carolina Press, 2004).

Oldham, James. *The Mansfield Manuscripts and the Growth of English Law in the Eighteenth Century*, vol. 1 (Chapel Hill: University of North Carolina Press, 1992).

Oldham, James. *The Mansfield Manuscripts and the Growth of English Law in the Eighteenth Century*, vol. 2 (Chapel Hill: University of North Carolina Press, 1992).

Shaw of Dunfermline, the Rt. Hon. Lord. "The Enlightenment of Lord Mansfield" (1926) 8 JCL & IL 1.

Shientag, Bernard L. "Lord Mansfield Revisited – A Modern Assessment" (1941) 10 Fordham L Rev 345.

References

Stephens, Charles. *The Jurisprudence of Lord Denning: A Study in Legal History*, vol. 1 (Newcastle upon Tyne: Cambridge Scholars, 2009).

Van Cleve, George. "*Somerset's Case* and Its Antecedents in Imperial Perspective" (2006) 24 LHR 601.

Waterman, Julian S. "Mansfield and Blackstone's Commentaries" (1933–1934) 1 U Chicago L Rev 549.

Secondary Sources: Websites and Wikipedia Entries

"Boroughbridge (UK Parliament constituency)," Wikipedia, http://en.wikipedia.org/wiki/Boroughbridge_(UK_Parliament_constituency).

"Colley Cibber," Wikipedia, http://en.wikipedia.org/wiki/Colley_Cibber.

"Court of King's Bench (England)," Wikipedia, http://en.wikipedia.org/wiki/Court_of_King's_Bench_(England).

"Exchequer of Pleas," Wikipedia, http://en.wikipedia.org/wiki/Exchequer_of_Pleas.

"Jacobitism," Wikipedia, http://en.wikipedia.org/wiki/Jacobitism.

"Lord Chief Justice of England and Wales," Wikipedia, http://en.wikipedia.org/wiki/Lord_Chief_Justice_of_England_and_Wales.

"Lord George Gordon," Wikipedia, http://en.wikipedia.org/wiki/Lord_George_Gordon.

"President of the Queen's Bench Division," Wikipedia, http://en.wikipedia.org/wiki/President_of_the_Queen's_Bench_Division.

"Somersett's Case," Wikipedia, http://en.wikipedia.org/wiki/Somersett's_Case.

"Thomas Pelham-Holles, 1st Duke of Newcastle," Wikipedia, http://en.wikipedia.org/wiki/Thomas_Pelham-Holles,_1st_Duke_of_Newcastle.

"William Blackstone," Wikipedia, http://en.wikipedia.org/wiki/William_Blackstone.

"William Murray, 1st Earl of Mansfield," Wikipedia, http://en.wikipedia.org/wiki/William_Murray,_1st_Earl_of_Mansfield.

"William Murray, Lord Mansfield," Westminster Abbey, http://www.westminster-abbey.org/our-history/people/william-murray,-lord-mansfield.

"William Pitt, 1st Earl of Chatham," Wikipedia, http://en.wikipedia
.org/wiki/William_Pitt,_1st_Earl_of_Chatham.

Cases

Carter v Boehm (1766), 3 Burr 1905, 97 ER 1162 (KB).

Chapman v Brown (1765), 3 Burr 1626, 97 ER 1015 (KB).

Eastwood v Kenyon (1840), 11 Ad & El 438, 113 ER 482 (KB).

Fisher v Prince (1762), 3 Burr 1363, 97 ER 876 (KB).

Hawkes v Saunders (1782), 1 Cowp 289, 98 ER 1091 (KB).

Jones v Randall (1774), 1 Cowp 37, 98 ER 954 (KB).

Luke v Lyde (1759), 2 Burr 882, 97 ER 614 (KB).

Millar v Taylor (1769), 4 Burr 2303, 98 ER 201 (KB).

Milles v Fletcher (1779), 1 Dougl 231, 99 ER 151 (KB).

Perrin v Blake (1770), 4 Burr 2579, 98 ER 355 (KB).

Pillans v Van Mierop (1765), 3 Burr 1663, 97 ER 1035 (KB).

Pugh v Duke of Leeds (1777), 2 Cowp 714, 98 ER 1323 (KB).

R v Woodfall (1770), 5 Burr 2661, 98 ER 398 (KB).

Somerset v Stewart (1772), Lofft 1, 98 ER 499 (KB).

Trueman v Fenton (1777), 2 Cowp 544, 98 ER 1232 (KB).

Tweddle v Atkinson (1861), 1 B & S 393, 121 ER 762 (KB).

Chapter 3. John Marshall: A Founding Judge

Secondary Sources: Books and Articles

Baker, Leonard. *John Marshall: A Life in Law* (New York: Macmillan, 1974).

Cuneo, John R. *John Marshall: Judicial Statesman* (New York: McGraw-Hill, 1975).

Dorfman, Joseph. "John Marshall: Political Economist" in W. Melville Jones, ed., *Chief Justice John Marshall: A Reappraisal* (New York: De Capo Press, 1971) 124.

Fairman, Charles. "John Marshall and the American Judicial Tradition" in W. Melville Jones, ed., *Chief Justice John Marshall: A Reappraisal* (New York: De Capo Press, 1971) 77.

Faulkner, Robert K. *The Jurisprudence of John Marshall* (Princeton, NJ: Princeton University Press, 1968).

References

Faulkner, Robert K. "The Marshall Court and the Making of Constitutional Democracy" in Thomas C. Shevory, ed., *John Marshall's Achievement: Law, Politics, and Constitutional Interpretations* (Westport, CT: Greenwood Press, 1989) 13.

Magruder, Allan B. *American Statesmen: John Marshall* (New York: Houghton, Mifflin, 1888).

Morgan, Donald G. "Marshall, the Marshall Court, and the Constitution" in W. Melville Jones, ed., *Chief Justice John Marshall: A Reappraisal* (New York: De Capo Press, 1971) 168.

Shevory, Thomas C. "Introduction" in Thomas C. Shevory, ed., *John Marshall's Achievement: Law, Politics, and Constitutional Interpretations* (Westport, CT: Greenwood Press, 1989) 1.

Simon, James F. *What Kind of Nation: Thomas Jefferson, John Marshall, and the Epic Struggle to Create a United States* (New York: Simon & Schuster, 2003).

Smith, Jean Edward. *John Marshall: Definer of a Nation* (New York: Henry Holt, 1996).

Swisher, Carl Brent. "Introduction" in W. Melville Jones, ed., *Chief Justice John Marshall: A Reappraisal* (New York: De Capo Press, 1971) 1.

Warren, Earl. "Foreword" in W. Melville Jones, ed., *Chief Justice John Marshall: A Reappraisal* (New York: De Capo Press, 1971) ix.

Secondary Sources: Websites and Wikipedia Entries

"John Marshall," Wikipedia, http://en.wikipedia.org/wiki/John_Marshall.

"John Marshall, 1801–1835," The Supreme Court Historical Society, http://www.supremecourthistory.org/history-of-the-court/chief-justices/john-marshall-1801–1835/.

"Thomas Jefferson," Wikipedia, http://en.wikipedia.org/wiki/Thomas_Jefferson.

Cases

Bracken v William and Mary, 7 Va 573 (Sup Ct 1790).
Fletcher v Peck, 10 US 87 (1810).

Gibbons v Ogden, 22 US 1 (1924).
Marbury v Madison, 5 US 137 (1803).
McCulloch v Maryland, 17 US 316 (1819).

Chapter 4. Oliver Wendell Holmes Jr.: The Magnificent Yankee

Secondary Sources: Books and Articles

Aichele, Gary J. *Oliver Wendell Holmes, Jr.: Soldier, Scholar, Judge* (Boston: Twayne, 1989).
Alschuler, Albert W. "The Descending Trail: Holmes' *Path of the Law* One Hundred Years Later" (1997) 49 Fla L Rev 353.
Alschuler, Albert W. *Law Without Values: The Life, Work, and Legacy of Justice Holmes* (Chicago: University of Chicago Press, 2000).
Bent, Silas. *Justice Oliver Wendell Holmes* (New York: Vanguard Press, 1932).
Holmes, Oliver Wendell, Jr. *The Common Law* (Cambridge, MA: Belknap Press of Harvard University Press, 2009).
Holmes, O. W. "The Path of the Law" (1897) 10 Harv L Rev 457.
Howe, Mark DeWolfe. *Justice Oliver Wendell Holmes: The Shaping Years, 1841–1870* (Cambridge, MA: Belknap Press, Harvard University Press, 1957).
Kellogg, Frederic R. *Oliver Wendell Holmes, Jr., Legal Theory, and Judicial Restraint* (New York: Cambridge University Press, 2007).
Lief, Alfred, ed. *The Dissenting Opinions of Mr. Justice Holmes* (New York: Vanguard Press, 1929).
Palmer, Ben W. "Hobbes, Holmes and Hitler" (1945) 31 ABA J 569.
Posner, Richard A., ed. *The Essential Holmes: Selections from the Letters, Speeches, Judicial Opinions, and Other Writings of Oliver Wendell Holmes, Jr.* (Chicago: University of Chicago Press, 1992).
Posner, Richard A., "Introduction" in Richard A. Posner, ed., *The Essential Holmes: Selections from the Letters, Speeches, Judicial Opinions, and Other Writings of Oliver Wendell Holmes, Jr.* (Chicago: University of Chicago Press, 1992).
Reimann, Mathias. "Horrible Holmes," Book Review of *Law Without Values: The Life, Work, and Legacy of Justice Holmes* by Albert W Alschuler (2001–2002) 100 Mich L Rev 1676.

References

White, G. Edward. *Oliver Wendell Holmes, Jr.* (New York: Oxford University Press, 2006).

Secondary Sources: Websites and Wikipedia Entries

"Oliver Wendell Holmes, Jr.," Wikipedia, http://en.wikipedia.org/wiki/Oliver_Wendell_Holmes,_Jr.

"Oliver Wendell Holmes, Sr.," Wikipedia, http://en.wikipedia.org/wiki/Oliver_Wendell_Holmes,_Sr.

Cases

Abrams v United States, 250 US 616 (1919).
Bailey v Alabama, 219 US 219 (1911).
Black & White Taxicab & Transfer v Brown & Yellow Taxicab & Transfer, 276 US 518 (1928).
Buck v Bell, 274 US 200 (1927).
Erie Railroad v Tompkins, 304 US 64 (1938).
Lochner v New York, 198 US 45 (1905).
Northern Securities Co. v United States, 193 US 197 (1904).
Schenck v United States, 249 US 47 (1919).

Chapter 5. James Atkin: An Ordinary Person

Secondary Sources: Books and Articles

Anonymous, "The Late Lord Atkin" (1945) 62 SALJ 55.
Gutteridge, H. C. "Lord Atkin of Aberdovey" (1945–1947) 9 Cambridge LJ 44.
Hadjihambis, D. "Mr. Justice Cardozo and Lord Atkin: A Comparative Study of the Judicial Process" (1978–1979) 12 Bracton LJ 147.
Harding, R. W. "Lord Atkin's Judicial Attitudes and Their Illustration in Commercial Law and Contract" (1964) 27 Mod L Rev 434.
Hutchinson, Allan C. *Is Eating People Wrong?: Great Legal Cases and How They Shaped the World* (New York: Cambridge University Press, 2011).
Lewis, Geoffrey. "Atkin, James Richard, Baron Atkin (1867–1944)" in *Oxford Dictionary of National Biography* (np: Oxford University

Press, 2004), Online Edition, http://www.oxforddnb.com/index/ 101030492/James-Atkin.

Lewis, Geoffrey. *Lord Atkin* (Portland, OR: Hart, 1999).

Samuels, Alec. "James Richard Atkin, Lord Atkin of Aberdovey" (1994) 25 Cambrian L Rev 147.

Wright, Lord. "In Memoriam, Lord Atkin of Aberdovey" (1944) 60 Law Q Rev 332.

Secondary Sources: Websites and Wikipedia Entries

"Gray's Inn | Scholarships – Pupillage," The Honourable Society of Gray's Inn, http://www.graysinn.info/index.php?option=com_ content&task=view&id=48&Itemid=58.

"James Atkin, Baron Atkin," Wikipedia, http://en.wikipedia.org/ wiki/Lord_Atkin.

Cases

Ambard v Attorney General for Trinidad and Tobago, [1936] AC 322.

Arcos v Ronaasen & Son, [1933] AC 470.

Bell v Lever Brothers Ltd., [1932] AC 161.

Everett v Griffiths, [1920] 3 KB 163.

IRC v Rossminster Ltd., [1980] AC 952.

Liversidge v Anderson, [1942] AC 206.

M'Alister (Donoghue) v Stevenson, [1932] AC 562.

Meering v Graham-White Aviation Co. Ltd., [1920] 122 LT 24 (CA).

Sim v Stretch, [1936] 2 All ER 1237 (HL).

Chapter 6. Tom Denning: An English Gardener

Secondary Sources: Books, Articles, and Multimedia

Denning, the Rt. Hon. Lord. *The Closing Chapter* (London: Butterworth, 1983).

Denning, the Rt. Hon. Lord. *The Discipline of Law* (London: Butterworth, 1979).

Denning, the Rt. Hon. Lord. *The Family Story* (London: Butterworth, 1981).

References

Denning, the Rt. Hon. Lord. *Freedom Under the Law* (London: Stevens & Sons, 1949).

Denning, the Rt. Hon. Lord. *What Next in the Law* (London: Butterworth, 1982).

Denning of Whitchurch, the Rt. Hon. Lord. *From Precedent to Precedent* (Oxford: Oxford University Press, 1959).

Denning, Alfred Thompson, Michael Doherty & David Hay, DVD: *A Conversation with Lord Denning* (Vancouver: Law Courts Education Society of BC, 1999).

Dyer, Clare. "Lord Denning, Controversial 'People's Judge,' Dies Aged 100" *The Guardian* (6 March 1999), http://www.guardian.co.uk/uk/1999/mar/06/claredyer1.

Freeman, Iris. *Lord Denning: A Life* (London: Hutchinson, Random House [UK], 1993).

Goff, Robert. "Denning, Alfred Thompson, Baron Denning (1899–1999)" in *Oxford Dictionary of National Biography* (np: Oxford University Press, 2004), Online Edition, http://www.oxforddnb.com/index/101072037/Alfred-Denning.

Griffith, J. A. G. Book Review of *The Discipline of Law* by Lord Denning (1979) 42 Mod L Rev 348.

Heward, Edmund. *Lord Denning: A Biography*, 2nd ed. (Chichester, UK: Barry Rose Law, 1997).

Heward, Edmund. "Obituaries: Lord Denning" *The Independent* (6 March 1999), http://www.independent.co.uk/arts-entertainment/obituaries-lord-denning-1078629.html.

Klinck, Dennis R. "'This Other Eden': Lord Denning's Pastoral Vision" (1994) 14 Oxford J Legal Stud 25.

"Lord Denning" *The Times* (15 November 2007), http://www.timesonline.co.uk/tol/comment/obituaries/article2876549.ece.

Sedley, Stephen. "A Benchmark of British Justice" *The Guardian* (6 March 1999), http://www.guardian.co.uk/news/1999/mar/06/guardianobituaries.

Stephens, Charles. *The Jurisprudence of Lord Denning: A Study in Legal History*, vol. 1 (Newcastle upon Tyne: Cambridge Scholars, 2009).

Wilson, A. N. "England, His England" *The Spectator* (18 August 1990).

Wilson, A. N. "If Only Lord Denning Had Died at Seventy..." *The Independent* (7 March 1999), http://www.independent.co.uk/opinion/if-only-lord-denning-had-died-at-seventy-1079046.html.

Secondary Sources: Websites and Wikipedia Entries

"Alfred Denning, Baron Denning," Wikipedia, http://en.wikipedia.org/wiki/Alfred_Denning,_Baron_Denning.

"Gavin Simonds, 1st Viscount Simonds," Wikipedia, http://en.wikipedia.org/wiki/Gavin_Simonds,_1st_Viscount_Simonds.

"Hon. Robert Gordon Denning," thePeerage.com, http://thepeerage.com/p23611.htm.

"Leon Brittan," Wikipedia, http://en.wikipedia.org/wiki/Leon_Brittan.

"Professor R.G. Denning," Oxford University Department of Chemistry, http://research.chem.ox.ac.uk/bob-denning.aspx.

Cases and Legislation

Beswick v Beswick, [1966] Ch 538, [1966] 3 All ER 1 (CA), aff'd, [1968] AC 58.

Broome v Cassell & Co. Ltd., [1971] 2 QB 354 (CA).

Candler v Crane, Christmas & Co., [1951] 2 KB 164 (CA).

Central London Property Trust Ltd. v High Trees House Ltd., [1947] KB 130.

Dutton v Bognor Regis Urban District Council, [1972] 1 QB 373 (CA).

Falmouth Boat Construction Co. Ltd. v Howell, [1950] 2 KB 16, aff'd [1951] AC 837.

Gallie v Lee, [1969] 2 Ch 17 (CA).

George Mitchell (Chesterhall) Ltd. v Finney Lock Seeds Ltd., [1983] QB 284 (CA).

Hedley Byrne & Co. Ltd. v Heller & Partners Ltd., [1964] AC 465.

Hinz v Berry, [1970] 2 QB 40 (CA).

Lamb v Camden London Borough Council, [1981] QB 625 (CA).

Lloyds Bank Ltd. v Bundy, [1975] QB 326 (CA).

Magor and St Mellons RDC v Newport Corp, [1950] 2 All ER 1226 (CA), aff'd [1952] AC 189.

References

M'Alister (Donoghue) v Stevenson, [1932] AC 562.

Mandla v Dowell Lea, [1983] QB 1 (CA), rev'd [1983] 2 AC 548.

Matrimonial Proceedings and Property Act 1970 (UK), c 45.

McIlkenny v Chief Constable of West Midlands Police Force, [1980] QB 283 (CA).

Sale of Goods Act 1979 (UK), c 54.

Ward v Bradford Co., [1972] 70 LGR 27 (CA).

Chapter 7. Thurgood Marshall: A Man on a Mission

Secondary Sources: Books and Articles

Ball, Howard. *A Defiant Life: Thurgood Marshall and the Persistence of Racism in America* (New York: Crown, 1998).

Bland, Randall W. *An Examination of the Legal Career of Thurgood Marshall Prior to His Elevation to the Supreme Court of the U.S., 1934–1967* (Ann Arbor, MI: University Microfilms, 1971).

Bland, Randall W. *Private Pressure on Public Law: The Legal Career of Justice Thurgood Marshall* (Port Washington, NY: Kennikat Press, 1973).

Bloch, Susan Low. "Foreword: Thurgood Marshall: Courageous Advocate, Compassionate Judge" (1992) 80 Geo LJ 2003.

Brennan, William. "Justice Thurgood Marshall: Advocate for Human Need in American Jurisprudence" (1981) 40 Md LR 390.

Brennan, William. "A Tribute to Justice Thurgood Marshall" (1991) 105 Harv L Rev 23.

Brennan, William J., Jr. "A Tribute to Justice Thurgood Marshall" in Roger Goldman & David Gallen, eds., *Thurgood Marshall: Justice for All* (New York: Carroll & Graf, 1992) 13.

Brown, Rebecca. "Deep and Wide: Justice Marshall's Contributions to Constitutional Law" (2009) 52 How LJ 637.

Darbyshire, Glen. "Clerking for Justice Marshall" in Roger Goldman & David Gallen, eds., *Thurgood Marshall: Justice for All* (New York: Carroll & Graf, 1992) 174.

Davis, Michael D. & Hunter R. Clark. *Thurgood Marshall: Warrior at the Bar, Rebel on the Bench* (New York: Carol Publishing Group, 1994).

Fisher, William W., III. "The Jurisprudence of Justice Marshall" (1989) 6 Harv BlackLetter LJ 131.

Gewirtz, Paul. "Thurgood Marshall" (1991) 101 Yale LJ 13.

Gewirtz, Paul. "Thurgood Marshall" in Roger Goldman & David Gallen, eds., *Thurgood Marshall: Justice for All* (New York: Carroll & Graf, 1992) 167.

Marshall, Thurgood. "The Constitution: A Living Document" in David M. O'Brien, ed., *Judges on Judging: Views from the Bench*, 3rd ed. (Washington, DC: CQ Press, 2009) 207.

Mello, Michael. *Against the Death Penalty: The Relentless Dissents of Justices Brennan and Marshall* (Boston: Northeastern University Press, 1996).

Minow, Martha. "Choices and Constraints: For Justice Thurgood Marshall" (1992) 80 Geo LJ 2093.

Minow, Martha. "A Tribute to Justice Thurgood Marshall" (1991) 105 Harv L Rev 66.

Minow, Martha. "A Tribute to Justice Thurgood Marshall" in Roger Goldman & David Gallen, eds., *Thurgood Marshall: Justice for All* (New York: Carroll & Graf, 1992) 180.

Rowan, Carl. *Dream Makers, Dream Breakers: The World of Justice Thurgood Marshall* (Toronto: Little, Brown, 1993).

Rowh, Mark. *Thurgood Marshall: Civil Rights Attorney and Supreme Court Justice* (Berkley Heights, NJ: Enslow, 2002).

Tushnet, Mark. "The Meritocratic Egalitarianism of Thurgood Marshall" (2009) 52 How LJ 691.

Tushnet, Mark V. *Making Constitutional Law: Thurgood Marshall and the Supreme Court, 1961–1991* (New York: Oxford University Press, 1997).

Williams, Juan. *Thurgood Marshall: American Revolutionary* (New York: Random House, 1998).

Williams, Karen Hastie. "Humanizing the Legal Process: The Legacy of Thurgood Marshall" (1989) 6 Harv BlackLetter LJ 90.

References

Cases

Brown v Board of Education of Topeka, 347 US 483 (1954).
Dandridge v Williams, 397 US 471 (1970).
Furman v Georgia, 408 US 238 (1972).
Murray v University of Maryland, 169 Md 478 (1936).
Patton v Mississippi, 332 US 463 (1947).
Regents v Bakke, 438 US 265 (1978).
Richmond, Virginia v JA Croson Co., 488 US 469 (1989).
Roe v Wade, 410 US 113 (1973).
San Antonio Independent School District v Rodriguez, 411 US 1 (1973).
Schneckloth v Bustamonte 412 US 218 (1973).
Shelly v Kraemer, 334 US 1 (1948).
Smith v Allwright, 321 US 649 (1944).
Stanley v Georgia, 394 US 557 (1969).
United States v Kras, 409 US 434 (1973).

Chapter 8. Bertha Wilson: Making the Difference

Secondary Sources: Books and Articles

Anderson, Ellen. *Judging Bertha Wilson: Law as Large as Life* (Toronto: University of Toronto Press for the Osgoode Society for Canadian Legal History, 2001).

Backhouse, Constance. "Justice Bertha Wilson and the Politics of Feminism" in Jamie Cameron, ed., *Reflections on the Legacy of Justice Bertha Wilson* (Markham, ON: LexisNexis, 2008) 33.

Belleau, Marie-Claire, Rebecca Johnson & Christina Vinters. "Voicing an Opinion: Authorship, Collaboration and the Judgments of Justice Bertha Wilson" in Jamie Cameron, ed., *Reflections on the Legacy of Justice Bertha Wilson* (Markham, ON: LexisNexis, 2008) 53.

Boyle, Christine. "The Role of the Judiciary in the Work of Madame Justice Wilson" (1992) 15 Dal LJ 241.

Brooks, Kim. "Introduction" in Kim Brooks, ed., *Justice Bertha Wilson: One Woman's Difference* (Vancouver: UBC Press, 2009) 1.

Bryden, Philip. "The Democratic Intellect: The State in the Work of Madame Justice Wilson" (1992) 15 Dal LJ 65.

Cameron, Jamie. "Justice in Her Own Right: Bertha Wilson and the Canadian Charter of Rights and Freedoms" in Jamie Cameron, ed., *Reflections on the Legacy of Justice Bertha Wilson* (Markham, ON: LexisNexis, 2008) 372.

Canadian Bar Association Task Force on Gender Equality in the Legal Profession, *Touchstones for Change: Equality, Diversity and Accountability* (Ottawa: Canadian Bar Association, 1993).

Dickson, Brian. "Madame Justice Wilson: Trailblazer for Justice" (1992) 15 Dal LJ 1.

Dodek, Adam. "The Dutiful Conscript: An Originalist View of Justice Wilson's Conception of Charter Rights and Their Limits" in Jamie Cameron, ed., *Reflections on the Legacy of Justice Bertha Wilson* (Markham, ON: LexisNexis, 2008) 331.

Fernandez, Angela & Beatrice Tice. "Bertha Wilson's Practice Years (1958–1975): Establishing a Research Practice and Founding a Research Department in Canada" in Kim Brooks, ed., *Justice Bertha Wilson: One Woman's Difference* (Vancouver: UBC Press, 2009) 15.

Halka, Elizabeth. "Madam Justice Bertha Wilson: A 'Different Voice' in the Supreme Court of Canada" (1996) 35 Alta L Rev 242.

Hawkins, Robert E. & Robert Martin. "Democracy, Judging and Bertha Wilson" (1995) 41 McGill LJ 1.

Kazan, Patricia. "Reasonableness, Gender Difference & Self-Defence Law" (1997) 24 Man LJ 549.

L'Heureux-Dubé, Claire. "Preface" in Kim Brooks ed., *Justice Bertha Wilson: One Woman's Difference* (Vancouver: UBC Press, 2009) ix.

MacPherson, James C. "Eulogy for Justice Bertha Wilson" in Jamie Cameron, ed., *Reflections on the Legacy of Justice Bertha Wilson* (Markham, ON: LexisNexis, 2008) xxix.

Mossman, Mary Jane. "'Contextualizing' Bertha Wilson: Wilson as a Woman in Law in Mid-20th Century Canada" in Jamie Cameron, ed., *Reflections on the Legacy of Justice Bertha Wilson* (Markham, ON: LexisNexis, 2008) 1.

Roach, Kent. "Justice Bertha Wilson: A Classically Liberal Judge" (2008) 41 Sup Ct L Rev (2d) 193.

References

Sharpe, Robert J. & Kent Roach. *Brian Dickson: A Judge's Journey* (Toronto: University of Toronto Press for the Osgoode Society for Canadian Legal History, 2003).

Supreme Court of Canada, News Release (30 April 2007), http://scc .lexum.org/en/news_release/2007/07–04–30/07–04–30.html.

Wilson, Bertha. "Decision Making in the Supreme Court" (1986) 36 UTLJ 227.

Wilson, Bertha. "My Years in the Court of Appeal, 1975–1982" (2001) 19 Advocates' Soc J 24.

Wilson, Bertha. "We Didn't Volunteer" (1999) 20 Policy Options 8.

Wilson, Bertha. "Will Women Judges Really Make a Difference?" (1990) 28 Osgoode Hall LJ 507.

Cases

Bhadauria v Board of Governors of Seneca College of Applied Arts and Technology (1979), 27 OR (2d) 142, 105 DLR (3d) 707 (CA).

Edmonton Journal v Alberta (Attorney General), [1989] 2 SCR 1326.

Guerin v The Queen, [1984] 2 SCR 335.

Pelech v Pelech, [1987] 1 SCR 801.

Pettkus v Becker (1978), 20 OR (2d) 105, 87 DLR (3d) 101 (CA).

R v Lavallee, [1990] 1 SCR 852.

R v Morgentaler, [1988] 1 SCR 30.

Shell Oil v Commissioner of Patents, [1982] 2 SCR 536.

Singh v Minister of Employment and Immigration, [1985] 1 SCR 177.

Vorvis v Insurance Co. of British Columbia, [1989] 1 SCR 1085.

Chapter 9. Albie Sachs: Of Struggles and Lies

Secondary Sources: Books and Articles

Bazelon, Emily. "After the Revolution" *Legal Affairs* (January/ February 2003), http://www.legalaffairs.org/issues/January-February-2003/feature_bazelon_janfeb2003.msp.

Bishop, Michael, Lisa Chamberlain & Sha'ista Kazee. "Twelve-Year Review of the Work of the Constitutional Court: A Statistical Analysis" (2008) 24 SAJHR 354.

Davis, Dennis. "The Law of Discovery and Intuition," Book Review of *The Strange Alchemy of Life and Law* by Albie Sachs, *Mail & Guardian* (23 April 2010), http://www.mg.co.za/article/2010–04–23-the-law-of-discovery-and-intuition.

Edgar, David. *The Jail Diary of Albie Sachs* in David Edgar, *Plays*, vol. 1 (London: Methuen Drama, 1997).

Ellmann, Stephen J. "Introduction: The Creation of South Africa's Constitution" (1996–1997) 41 NYL Sch L Rev 665.

Forsyth, John. "Albie Sachs Interview: A Peek inside the Mind of Those Who Sit in Judgment" *Edinburgh Daily News* (29 June 2009), http://news.scotsman.com/world/Albie-Sachs-interview-A-peek.5408972.jp.

Hills, Carol. "Sachs Tells How He Crafted ANC's Code of Conduct" *Mail & Guardian* (9 November 2007), http://www.mg.co.za/article/2007–11–09-sachs-tells-how-he-crafted-ancs-code-of-conduct.

Lenta, Patrick. "The Literary Judge" (2007) 18 Stellenbosch L Rev 313.

Ménager-Everson, S. V. "The Albie Sachs Debate" (1992) 23:4 Res. in African Lit. 59.

Oder, Norman. "Albie Sachs: Hope for Soft Vengeance in South Africa" (1992) 14:1 American Lawyer 86.

Quattrocchi, Allison. "Justice Under a Tree: The Inspiration Behind a South Africa Court Building" (2010) 46 Ariz Att'y 16.

Roberts, Ronald Suresh. "Law and Dogma: The Illiberal Elite" *Mail & Guardian* (23 October 2009), http://www.mg.co.za/article/2009–10–23-law-and-dogma-the-illiberal-elite.

Sachs, Albie. *Advancing Human Rights in South Africa* (Cape Town: Oxford University Press, 1992).

Sachs, Albie. "Albie Sachs: 'The Fact that South Africa Is a Country at All Is One of the Greatest Stories of Our Time'" *The Guardian* (16 May 2010), http://www.guardian.co.uk/culture/2010/may/16/albie-sachs-south-africa-world-cup.

References

Sachs, Albie. *The Free Diary of Albie Sachs* (Johannesburg: Random House, 2004).

Sachs, Albie. *The Jail Diary of Albie Sachs* (London: Harvill Press, 1966).

Sachs, Albie. "Judges and Gender: The Constitutional Rights of Women in a Post-Apartheid South Africa" (1990) 7 Agenda 1.

Sachs, Albie. *The Soft Vengeance of a Freedom Fighter*, 2nd ed. (Berkeley, Los Angeles: University of California Press, 2000).

Sachs, Albie. *Stephanie on Trial* (London: Harvill Press, 1968).

Sachs, the Hon. Albie. "The Creation of South Africa's Constitution" (1996–1997) 41 NYL Sch L Rev 669.

Sachs, Justice Albie. *The Strange Alchemy of Life and Law* (New York: Oxford University Press, 2009).

Sachs, Justice Albie. "Tolerance in a Time of Cholera" (Address delivered at the Cape Town Press Club, 22 April 2010), Cape Town Press Club, http://www.capetownpc.org.za/docs/speeches/tolerance-in-a-time-of-cholera.pdf.

Scheper-Hughes, Nancy. "Introduction to the New Edition – Sacred Wounds: Writing with the Body" in Albie Sachs, *The Soft Vengeance of a Freedom Fighter*, 2nd ed. (Berkeley, Los Angeles: University of California Press, 2000).

Steinberg, Carol. "Albie Sachs: Our Shakespearean Fool" (1991) 35:1 The Drama Review 194.

Tutu, Desmond. "Foreword to the New Edition" in Albie Sachs, *The Soft Vengeance of a Freedom Fighter*, 2nd ed. (Berkeley, Los Angeles: University of California Press, 2000).

Woolf, Harry. "Preface" in Justice Albie Sachs, *The Strange Alchemy of Life and Law* (New York: Oxford University Press, 2009).

Secondary Sources: Websites, Wikipedia Entries, and Other Media

"Albie Sachs," Academy of Achievement, http://www.achievement.org/autodoc/page/sac0bio-1.

"Albie Sachs," Wikipedia, http://en.wikipedia.org/wiki/Albie_Sachs.

"Albie Sachs: The Strange Alchemy of Life and Law – A Conversation with Albie Sachs, Jack Greenberg and Aryeh Neier" (Video interview, Open Society Institute, 21 January 2010), FORA.tv, http://fora.tv/2010/01/21/Albie_Sachs_The_Strange_Alchemy_of_Life_and_Law.

"Constitutional Court of South Africa," Wikipedia, http://en.wikipedia.org/wiki/Constitutional_court_of_south_africa.

"Daniel François Malan," Wikipedia, http://en.wikipedia.org/wiki/Daniel_François_Malan.

"Judge Albert Louis 'Albie' Sachs," South African History Online, http://www.sahistory.org.za/people/judge-albert-louis-albie-sachs.

"Landmark Cases," Constitutional Court of South Africa, http://www.constitutionalcourt.org.za/site/thecourt/history.htm#cases.

"Moses Kotane," Wikipedia, http://en.wikipedia.org/wiki/Moses_Kotane.

Ostroff, Maurice. "An Open Letter to Judge Albie Sachs," http://maurice-ostroff.tripod.com/id273.html.

Constitutional Court Statistical Analyses (by Year)

1995: Klaaren, Jonathan. "Statistics: Constitutional Court Statistics for the 1995 Term" (1996) 12 SAJHR 39.

1996: Klaaren, Jonathan. "Statistics: Constitutional Court Statistics for the 1996 Term" (1997) 13 SAJHR 208.

1997: Taylor, Lynn & Jonathan Klaaren. "Statistics: Constitutional Court Statistics for the 1997 Term" (1998) 14 SAJHR 277.

1998: Klaaren, Jonathan et al. "Constitutional Court Statistics for the 1998 Term" (1999) 15 SAJHR 256.

"Erratum Note: Constitutional Court Statistics 1998" (1999) 15 SAJHR 446.

1999: Leuta, Allen et al. "Constitutional Court Statistics for the 1999 Term" (2000) 16 SAJHR 364.

2000: Budlender, Steven et al. "Constitutional Court Statistics for the 2000 Term" (2001) 17 SAJHR 277.

References

2001: Teichner, Shaun et al. "Constitutional Court Statistics for the 2001 Term" (2002) 18 SAJHR 463.

2002: Klaaren, Jonathan et al. "Constitutional Court Statistics for the 2002 Term" (2003) 19 SAJHR 506.

2003: Klaaren, Jonathan et al. "Constitutional Court Statistics for the 2003 Term" (2004) 20 SAJHR 491.

2004: Klaaren, Jonathan, Nikki Stein & Carolina Nomphumelelo Xulu. "Constitutional Court Statistics for the 2004 Term" (2005) 21 SAJHR 636.

2005: Bishop, Michael et al. "Constitutional Court Statistics for the 2005 Term" (2006) 22 SAJHR 518.

Cases and Legislation

August and Another v Electoral Commission and Others, [1999] ZACC 3, [1999] 4 B Const LR 363.

Constitution of the Republic of South Africa, No 200 of 1993 as repealed by Constitution of the Republic of South Africa, 1996, No 108 of 1996.

Constitution of the Republic of South Africa, 1996, No 108 of 1996.

Kaunda and Others v President of the Republic of South Africa, [2004] ZACC 5, [2004] 10 B Const LR 1009.

Minister of Home Affairs and Another v Fourie and Another, [2005] ZACC 19, [2006] 3 B Const LR 355.

Minister of Home Affairs (Bermuda) v Fisher and Another, [1980] AC 319, [1979] 3 All ER 21, [1979] 2 WLR 889 PC (Eng).

Mistry v Interim National Medical and Dental Council and Others, [1998] ZACC 10, [1998] 7 B Const LR 880.

Prinsloo v Van der Linde and Another, [1997] ZACC 5, [1997] 6 B Const LR 759.

S v Baloyi and Others, [1999] ZACC 19, [2000] 1 B Const LR 86.

S v Basson, [2005] ZACC 10, [2005] 12 B Const LR 1192.

S v Lawrence; S v Negal; S v Solberg, [1997] ZACC 11, [1997] 10 B Const LR 1348.

S v Mhlungu and Others, [1995] ZACC 4, [1995] 7 B Const LR 793.

Chapter 10. Judging the Future: A Leap in the Dark

Secondary Sources: Books and Articles

Melville, Herman. "Hawthorne and His *Mosses*" *The Literary World* 7:185 (17 August 1850) 125.

Melville, Herman. "Hawthorne and His *Mosses*" *The Literary World* 7:186 (24 August 1850) 145.

Pope, Alexander. *An Essay on Man*, ed. by Frank Brady (New York: Macmillan, 1988).

Stephen, James Fitzjames. *Liberty, Equality, Fraternity* (Indianapolis: Liberty Fund, 1993).

Index

Index

Index

Index

Index

Index

Index

Index

Index